THE FIRST ARTISTS

THE
FIRST ARTISTS

By Dorothy and Joseph Samachson

World's Work Ltd
The Windmill Press, Kingswood, Tadworth, Surrey

PUBLISHER'S NOTE
In this edition of *The First Artists* one billion
equals one thousand million (1,000,000,000).

Designed by Abigail S. Moseley

Copyright © 1970 by Dorothy and Joseph Samachson
All rights reserved
First published in Great Britain 1973 by
World's Work Ltd
The Windmill Press
Kingswood, Tadworth, Surrey

Printed by offset in Great Britain by
William Clowes & Sons, Limited
London, Beccles and Colchester

SBN 437 15425 4

For
Dr. Lewis P. (Bud) Rowland and Dr. Stanley Fahn
With Affection and Gratitude

CONTENTS

Wadi Sora, Libyan Desert. This painting of the hand and men may have been a ritual fresco with a religious meaning. The modern viewer is awed by the power of the great hand and the beauty of the design.

INTRODUCTION

The rock art of prehistoric man is found around the world.

In the caves of France and Spain, in the rocky deserts of north Africa, and on the crags of Norwegian fjords, thousands of rock paintings and carvings have been discovered. Sometimes the astonishment of the discoverers has been so great that they have refused to believe the evidence of their own eyes. However, after years of bitter argument, archaeologists and anthropologists have agreed that these paintings and carvings were the work of prehistoric, primitive men, and that they were first created about twenty thousand years ago. Some are still being created at the present time, for man has remained prehistoric for different lengths of time in different places, as we shall see later.

Apparently, all the artists, no matter where or when they lived, belonged to the same species of man—named *Homo sapiens,* or wise man, to distinguish him from prehistoric species less capable than his own. As the designation *prehistoric* is usually taken to refer to times before *written* history, students of prehistoric archaeology, by definition, cannot learn about prehistoric man from ancient documents or inscriptions.

Nevertheless, before rupestral, or rock, art was discovered, archaeologists had already acquired, by examining the remains of ancient bones and implements, a considerable amount of information about the food prehistoric man ate, and the tools and weapons he used. Some archaeologists had convinced themselves that they already knew most of the important facts about him, and that further discoveries would merely fill in the gaps in their knowledge, without offering great surprises.

Although the discovery of rock art has filled in many gaps, it has at the same time created new and disquieting mysteries. Could prehistoric man of twenty thousand years ago really paint as well as some of the pictures indicated? Not all the paintings are masterpieces, but there are masterpieces among them. As the archaeologist, Gabriel de Mortillet, said, it was the Childhood of Art, but not the Art of Children. How did prehistoric man learn to paint with such skill so long before Raphael and Michelangelo? How did he form his images of clay and stone thousands of years before the great Greek sculptors, Praxiteles and Phidias?

Equally puzzling is another question: Why did ancient man paint at all? What on earth possessed him to penetrate deep into the darkness of a cave where he had to work in a cramped corner by the light of flickering lamps or torches, or build scaffolding to reach the ceiling? Some of his painted caves resemble the walls of a modern art gallery, but why put a gallery where his viewers would have so much trouble reaching it?

At a period when the struggle for life against the elements, against predatory animals, against hunger, was so constant and bitter, why should he waste his time laboriously engraving an open rock near the Arctic Circle? Did he, perhaps, paint for pleasure? Was this a case of art for art's sake?

In the following pages, we shall consider some of the answers that have been suggested to these questions. But first, let us look at the world in which the artists lived and see how it differed from our own.

THE FIRST ARTISTS

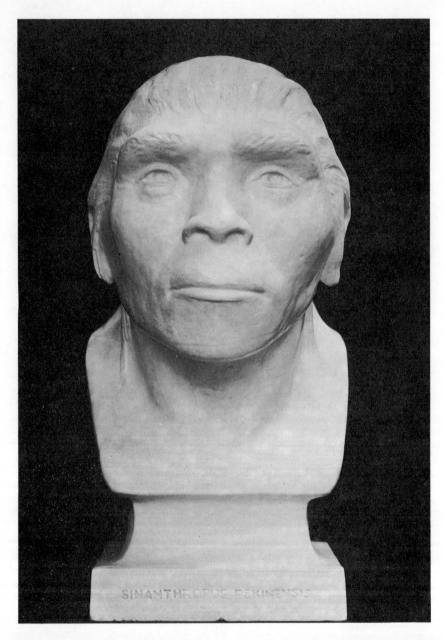

A plaster cast reconstruction of Peking man who lived in caves and used fire about a half million years ago.

ONE

OF ICE AND MEN

The earth is more than four billion years old. During the early part of this unimaginably vast stretch of time it developed its present approximately spherical shape, and its atmosphere changed slowly from a mixture of various gases, including such poisonous ones as hydrogen cyanide, to one that contained free oxygen, a gas needed by most forms of life. As the millions of years went by, oceans and continents formed and life began to trace a long and tortuous path from a submicroscopic complex of chemicals, first to genuine cells, and eventually to present-day plants and animals.

Of these four billion years, it is only the last one or two million that concern us here. This period, known as the *Pleistocene,* or most recent, saw a good part of the transition from ancient manlike apes to more or less apelike men.

The oldest remains of bones and teeth that we might classify as human, or at least as much human as apelike, date to about a million B.C. or earlier. Found in south Africa, these bones and tooth fragments belonged to a creature called *Australopithecus,* southern ape. Tools made of pebbles have been found among his remains, but it is not certain that he made them. If he did, he should be considered sufficiently intelligent to be classified as more man than ape.

On skipping several hundred thousand years we encounter a small number of fossil types, more advanced than *Australopithecus.* Skeletal fragments found in the island of Java are definitely manlike, and are ascribed to "Java man," also known as *Pithecanthropus erectus,* erect ape man. And about a half million years ago (the dates are highly uncertain), Lan-t'ien man and Peking man flourished in China. While man was slowly spreading through Africa and Asia, he was also evolving in Europe. But here the picture was complicated by the invasion of cold and ice.

During the Pleistocene period, the Northern Hemisphere knew four great ice ages, long periods of time during which the surface of northern Europe, the North American continent, and northern Asia were covered by great sheets of ice, in some places reaching a thickness of many thousand feet. The ice advanced or retreated slowly from century to century, and occasionally, after about twenty or forty thousand years, withdrew to give the land a temporary respite. Whenever the ice loosened its grip, animal and plant life sprang up on the soil set free. There were three long interglacial periods in the Pleistocene and many short ones, and it was during the respites from cold and ice that much of the European evolution and development of man took place. Among the types that flourished during this period were Swanscombe man, so called because his remains were found in Swanscombe, England, and Steinheim man, in Germany. Both types developed at about the same time as Java man and Peking man (give or take a couple of hundred thousand years).

We have so few remains that date so far back that the discovery of a new site where early man lived during this period can yield remarkable discoveries. In 1965 such a site was found in Nice, in the south of France. Excavation showed that men had lived here about three hundred thousand years ago and had constructed oval huts, some of them almost fifty feet long, out of wooden stakes. These huts are the oldest known dwellings constructed by human hands.

A more modern type, Neanderthal man, whose remains were first dug up in the Neander Valley in Germany in 1856, appeared about seventy-five thousand years ago. Neanderthal man turned out to have a much greater range than any of the types mentioned so far. Additional Neanderthal skeletons, together with some objects he created, have been found in many parts of Europe and Asia among the deposits of soil, rocks, and vegetation laid down between the third and fourth glacial periods.

From measurements made on all the skeletons available, we know that Neanderthal man was short, with an average height of about five feet. He had a long and exceptionally full face, with deep-set eyes and a thick but receding jaw. His body was strong, and his chest broad and deep. His brain was almost as large as that of the modern European, but certain areas of the brain were smaller and less complex.

The average person who has heard of Neanderthal man pictures him as a brutal caveman, holding a large club in his hand, and often dragging along by the hair his almost equally brutal mate. It seems incredible that this shambling apelike creature could have had any intellectual and spiritual life. But the evidence is that he was not shambling or apelike and that he thought much as we do. He was a skilled toolmaker, and must have had a good knowledge of nature in order to remain alive for so many generations in so dangerous a world as his was. He believed in some sort of survival after death, for when he buried his dead, in many cases he buried along with them gifts that they might use in their afterlife. Whether because of his religious beliefs or for other reasons, he showed consideration of the aged and infirm, for some of the Neanderthal skeletons found in burial sites have shown signs of age and illness which would imply that such people were not done away with as burdens to the community.

Some archaeologists now classify him as *Homo sapiens Neanderthalis,* or as *Homo presapiens,* man before wise man.

At the peak of his development during late Pleistocene time, Neanderthal man was found in relativley great numbers in Europe, Africa, Palestine, and central Asia. Then he disappeared from the fossil record. His extinction may have been due to one or more of a number of causes. He may have been isolated during a glacial period in an

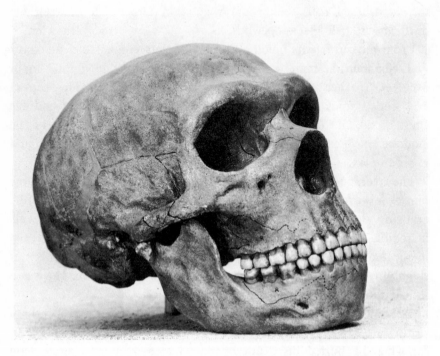

Neanderthal skull. Compare the head shape with that of Cro-Magnon man.

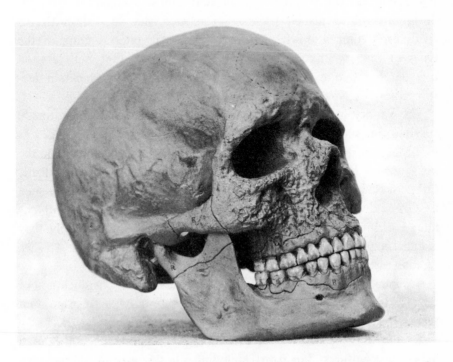

Cro-Magnon skull. Note the great evolutionary leap from Neanderthal man in forehead, teeth, lower jaw, and general shape.

area where the animals he hunted had decreased in number. He may have been unable to adapt to the intense cold. His slightly smaller brain may have put him at a disadvantage against other types of *Homo sapiens,* who seem to have arrived from the east during an interglacial period. Whether Neanderthal man was killed off, died out during the bitter glacial periods, or existed side by side with his rivals for a time and whether there was some intermingling of the types of man is unknown. Most scientists doubt that both existed together for a long period, although some fossil bones contain features of both Neanderthal and other *Homo sapiens.*

The variety of *Homo sapiens* that became the victor and ultimate survivor of what may have been many centuries of struggle was Cro-Magnon man, who like other prehistoric men, is named for the place where his skeleton was first found, Cro-Magnon, in France. Other skeletal remains of *Homo sapiens* have also been found, such as Grimaldi man, in Italy. Apparently, all types of *Homo sapiens* mated with each other, and all resembled modern man. Finally they reached a period in man's prehistory in which only a single species of man existed.

Archaeologists have found it useful to develop a classification of their own, quite distinct from the classification by soil strata that serves the geologists. This is classification by *cultures.*

To the anthropologist and archaeologist, all societies of human beings are cultures, the word including all the aspects of the way people live—the superstitions they have, the clothes they wear, the food they eat, and the tools they use. We know the ideas and beliefs of prehistoric man only by inference from the clues he left behind, a few of which have survived until archaeologists could study them. We are also severely limited in our knowledge of his daily life. But we know something of his eating habits, thanks to patient examination of his kitchen refuse for bones, shells, and other material objects that have been able to resist centuries of attack by wind and rain. Usually, however, we can depend most on our knowledge of ancient prehistoric tools and weapons, for these were made at first of stone and later of copper and bronze, and stone and metals usually endured thousands of years of weathering and decay better than the other materials prehistoric man used.

Cultures are usually named after the geographical sites where they were first discovered. It must again be emphasized that they have no direct connection with geological classification, although a knowledge of the geology of the place of discovery is often very useful.

Above all other geological influences on the prehistory of man in Europe was the impact of the different ice ages. The enormous sheets of ice not only made it impossible for man and the animals he hunted to live where they covered the soil, they changed geography on a grand scale. They lowered the sea level on the European coast by hundreds of feet when they locked up tremendous quantities of ice, and raised it again when the ice melted. They created oceans of ice on land when the temperature dropped, only to transform them into great fresh water seas in central Europe and Siberia when the temperature rose again. And they influenced the climate of all of Europe, for even where the ice could not penetrate, cold north winds did. In this way, the ice sheets provided a means of natural selection, determining both the plant life that could grow in its shadow and the animals that could live on the plants.

For good or bad, *Homo sapiens* would not be what he is today if not for the ice ages.

A portion of the ceiling at Altamira. The artists utilized the rocky protuber-
ances to give the animals a three-dimensional quality. This is lost in the two
dimensions of the photograph, and the animals appear distorted.

TWO

THE CAVE OF ALTAMIRA

"Look, Papa, the bulls!" With these words, a five-year-old girl announced the discovery in the cave of Altamira of the memorable paintings that were to turn the world of archaeology upside down.

Don Marcelino, Marquis de Sautuola, the "papa" to whom she called, was a cultured, well-to-do Spanish aristocrat with both an intense interest in archaeology and the intelligence to realize his limitations as an amateur. He had known of the cave for about a dozen years, learning of it from the report of a fox hunter, whose dog had been trapped among some rocks. On moving the rocks, the hunter found the entrance to an unknown cave. Although the discovery served at first as an occasional subject for conversation, it was soon forgotten, for this area of Spain, the province of Santander, was full of caves, and the cave of Altamira did not seem of particular interest.

As time passed, Don Marcelino's interest in caves grew. Archaeologists had begun to explore caves in France and other European countries and had uncovered a small number of bones belonging to early human types, along with a much greater number of *artifacts*, as they called objects made by man. Don Marcelino began to think of doing some exploring of his own—and what better place was there to start than right at home, in the cave of Altamira?

Among his earliest discoveries, made by lamp and candlelight in 1875 shortly after he began work, were a few faint drawings of animals in the walls of the first chamber of the cave. These were not spectacular examples of art, and although he reported that he had discovered drawings made by ancient cave dwellers, his report aroused little interest.

Don Marcelino continued to dig, sifting slowly through the layers of soil that had accumulated through hundreds of generations. He found, as he had hoped, flints that might have been used as implements and weapons, along with animal bones, some of them engraved. They provided unmistakable evidence that the cave had been used by ancient Stone Age men. A visit to the Paris International Exhibition of 1878 turned out to be unexpectedly rewarding. Here he met a well-known archaeologist, Dr. Edouard Piètte, whose views on prehistory were interesting and unorthodox. For one thing, Dr. Piètte held that man had existed for much longer than most of his fellow archaeologists believed. Stimulated by Dr. Piètte's ideas about the possible age of man on earth, and better informed about excavation techniques, Don Marcelino returned to Spain, prepared to work alone for years in this vast cavern near his home.

His solitude was broken only when he brought along his daughter, Maria. She was a well-behaved child, and could be trusted not to wander off and get lost. Moreover, she had the satisfaction of engaging in the same adult pursuits as her father. While he, as it seemed to her, played with dirt hour after hour in the vestibule, she did the same only thirty feet from the entrance, in a nearby chamber that was connected by passageways and tunnels to other large chambers.

It was in 1879 that she looked up at the ceiling and made her great discovery of the bulls. Without her, Don Marcelino might have discovered them eventually, but only with considerable luck, for the ceiling of the cave varied in height from four to seven feet above

Stone Age tools. The cruder one at the right is Magdalenian, about 15,000 B.C., the period of heroic art. The others are Neolithic, several thousand years later.

the floor, and Don Marcelino, who had to stoop where the ceiling was low, had been looking only at the floor of the cave.

Don Marcelino followed where Maria pointed and stared in astonishment. Groups of animals painted on the ceiling seemed to leap at him. Animals were painted in various positions: running, standing, even seated. Prominent among them were the great bison that Maria had called "bulls," but there were also wild boars, deer, and horses painted in red, brown, yellow, and black, all with the skill and strength of a master artist. Some of the paintings seemed to have been painted over earlier ones, and some had been engraved first with sharp chiseling tools. The outcroppings of rock on the ceiling had also been utilized to give the paintings a three-dimensional appearance. He knew at once that he had made an important discovery.

Most of the animals were from five to six feet in length, a far cry from the small-scale engravings on bone that he had dug up. Among the paintings, however, were several figures which were not clearly decipherable. Upon close examination he saw that they had a human posture, but no other recognizable human aspects. There were, in addition, abstract geometric designs now called *tectiforms*.

The chamber itself was sixty feet long and twenty-seven feet wide. During the next few days, Don Marcelino explored the cave more carefully, this time examining both walls and ceilings and making measurements. The entire cave was nine hundred feet long, penetrating deep into a limestone cliff. The other chambers, which were connected by various passageways and tunnels, also contained painted and engraved figures of animals, as well as handprints, lines drawn with fingers, probably in wet clay, and what appeared to be bear tracks. In all, the cave contained about 150 figures.

As works of art, many of the paintings were magnificent. They were best seen when the viewer lay down on the floor of the cave and looked upward. In this respect they brought to mind the Sistine Chapel in the Vatican, which had been painted by Michelangelo. Here, too, the artist had worked under difficult conditions, crawling along a scaffolding that brought him close to the ceiling, his muscles cramped by his awkward position, his eyes bleary from peering at his work in a dim and uncertain light. No wonder that the archaeologist, Joseph Déchellette, when he finally saw the great cham-

A bison on the wall of Altamira. Another animal may be seen in the upper left.

ber at Altamira, called it the Sistine Chapel of Quaternary Art. (The Quaternary is another name for approximately the same geological period we now call the Pleistocene.)

For the study of man, the implications of the paintings were tremendous. The bison, despite the fact that Maria had called them bulls, were not exactly like any animals that now live in Spain. Neither were the deer, the boars, or the horses. The meaning of this fact was clear: the paintings had been done thousands of years ago, while these ancient animals still roamed through northern Spain— done, therefore, by prehistoric men.

When Don Marcelino touched the paintings with careful fingers, they felt slightly greasy. What the grease had been, whether animal or vegetable, he did not know. But it had evidently protected the pigments from destruction by air and moisture over the centuries.

Don Marcelino knew that his discoveries in the cave were contrary to the theories of human development then accepted. Men who still used flints for weapons and tools were supposed to have been too brutish and too ignorant to learn the secrets of finding pigments and mixing colors, let alone to paint with such skill.

Well aware that he now needed professional aid and advice, de Don Marcelino immediately reported what he had found to Dr. Vilanova y Piera, a Spanish geologist. Dr. Vilanova, after examining both the paintings and the cave, was also convinced of the antiquity of the paintings, and he delivered a lecture about the discovery, expressing his belief that these paintings were from the upper Paleolithic, the last period of the Old Stone Age, beginning about 40,000 B.C., a time when no human beings with such accomplishments had been believed to exist. (This estimate has been challenged by modern archaeologists who, on the basis of new scientific evidence, believe that most of the art of Altamira was executed sometime between 15,000 to 12,000 B.C.)

As news of the paintings spread, the cave became the center of world-wide attention. Among the hundreds of visitors who came to marvel at Altamira was the king of Spain, who graciously outlined his name on the walls of the cave with the smoke of a burning candle.

In 1880, however, a congress of prehistoric archaeology was held in Lisbon and the findings at Altamira were rejected. Members of the congress had originally planned to inspect the caves themselves. Then they decided that an examination of reproductions of the paintings was enough; it was clear that the paintings were fraudulent.

Articles attacking the authenticity of the discoveries of Altamira began to appear. One archaeologist finally did visit the cave and examined the paintings, only to put a final stamp of rejection on them.

Don Marcelino had published a book about the cave, describing his finds, but this, too, was ridiculed. At several scholarly meetings that he attended, he was not permitted to speak in his own defense.

Don Marcelino died in 1888, unable to the end to clear his name of the charges of forgery and fraud. In 1889 at an international congress of archaeologists in Paris, Altamira was not even mentioned. Both the town and the cave returned to their former sleepy obscurity.

Hall of Bison at Niaux in southeastern France. A large cave consisting of several galleries, it ranks with Altamira and Lascaux as one of the richest storehouses of Magdalenian art. The detail below shows a bison and an ibex pierced with arrows or spears.

THREE

ALTAMIRA: AFTERMATH

Today, even the layman feels superior to the rigid-minded archaeologists who attacked the discoveries at Altamira with scorn and
derision. It is all too easy to forget how difficult it is, even in science,
to accept the validity of facts that contradict our own beliefs.

Archaeologists had good reason to be skeptical about sensational
new finds, for they were only too well acquainted with forgery and
fraud. All over the world, but principally in Europe, collectors had
for centuries bought frauds of all kinds, from artificially aged statues
and objects of art to forged paintings signed with the names of
Rembrandt, Rubens, and other artists long dead. Only two decades
before Don Marcelino's discovery of the art of Altamira, students and
workmen of the French archaeologist, Boucher de Perthes, "salted"
excavations with flint implements that they knew their master would
be eager to find. Exposure of the fraud, which was not long in coming,
not only clouded de Perthes' reputation, but created an atmosphere
of doubt about important discoveries in general.

The most notorious fraud in all archaeology came long after the Altamira episode had ended; it found many archaeologists accepting the validity of "Piltdown man," a creature whose existence was deduced from a collection of bone and tooth fragments supposedly found near Piltdown, in England. Piltdown man was "discovered" in 1912 and was not definitely revealed as a fraud until 1953, although some archaeologists had their doubts from the beginning.

Piltdown man was accepted by so many scientists as valid simply because the bones and teeth supported their ideas about the evolution of man. It was eventually rejected because scientists' ideas about evolution had changed, and the existence of this peculiar man ape contradicted the new ideas and led to a complete investigation.

Time was in the long run on the side of Don Marcelino. His enemies were growing older and were being replaced by younger, more open-minded men.

Moreover, as the nineteenth century drew to a close, paintings like those at Altamira were discovered in other caves both in Spain and in France, and the archaeologists who had attacked the paintings at Altamira became confused and unhappy men. *All* these magnificent paintings could not be frauds. It was ridiculous to imagine that some anonymous artist had invented a cave style and was now racing from one cave to another in order to paint forged masterpieces.

The nature of the new paintings and the situations in which some of them were found argued unanswerably against fraud. In 1895, the archaeologist Rivière, while working in La Mouthe, a cave in the Dordogne region of France, noticed murals *under* deposits of minerals on the walls. The deposits were obviously many centuries old; no modern artist could have created the paintings under them. Examination of other caves revealed similar situations. And in 1901 three archaeologists discovered some splendid cave art in Les Combarelles, in the same region of France.

Don Marcelino's enemies were becoming ever more doubtful of their own conclusions. In 1903, Emile Cartailhac, the archaeologist who had led the attack on the authenticity of Altamiran art, came to Altamira with a young student, Henri Breuil. Their thorough study of the paintings removed all doubts. The paintings at Altamira were obviously genuine, and the cave itself was a magnificent museum of Paleolithic man's accomplishments, miraculously preserved from destruction.

Cartailhac published a paper, "Mea Culpa d'un Sceptique," *The Guilt of a Skeptic,* in which he admitted that Don Marcelino had been essentially right and he himself wrong. In his grave, Don Marcelino was vindicated, and his daughter, Maria, now a grown woman, had the sad satisfaction of seeing his name and reputation restored to a place of honor.

With this auspicious beginning, young Henri Breuil, better known as the Abbé Breuil, went on to become the world's greatest expert on cave paintings. Archaeology owes him a great debt. But as might be expected, in later years the weight of his authority began to stifle archaeological thought, and he was in turn challenged by younger men, among them some of his own students.

The dog and two boys who discovered Lascaux.

FOUR

FRANCO-CANTABRIAN ART

The cave of Altamira contains the most famous parietal, or wall, prehistoric art in the world, but it is far from being the only one of its kind. Throughout northern Spain and in several provinces of France there are caves that house magnificent galleries of paintings. On the same artistic level as Altamira is Lascaux, in France. Its story is not so sensational as that of Altamira, but there is a strong similarity in the circumstances that led to its discovery in 1940— the wanderings of a dog among the rocks, and the search for it by its young masters. Still other caves and cave art have been discovered since then, Cougnac and Rouffignac, both in France, being found in the 1950s. The authenticity of the art in Rouffignac was for a time seriously questioned, since the cave itself had been occupied by the German Nazi invaders during World War II and later by the French partisans. Some archaeologists thought that these modern cave dwellers had created the paintings. However, the art was finally accepted. A sixteenth-century document that referred to the cave

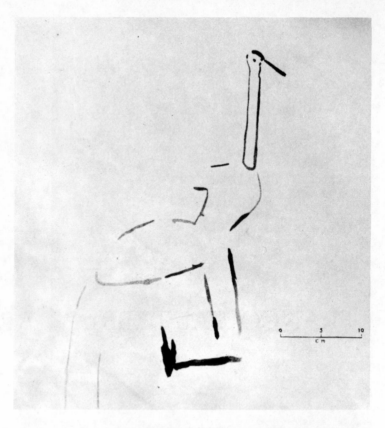

Copy by the archaeologist of an unidentified birdlike creature from Escoural, Portugal. The pictures in this cave are partly hidden by layers of calcified deposits produced by water seepage through the rocks for thousands of years, and only traces of the original paintings have survived.

and condemned its paintings as the work of evil spirits played an important part in proving the art to be authentic.

In 1963 a dynamite blast by a quarrying crew exposed a cave in Escoural, Portugal. Archaeologists have begun a study of the pictures and artifacts there and will be occupied for many years.

Although much of the cave art was discovered by accident, archaeologists have become increasingly active in their search for it. Guided by local folklore, they have made a systematic examination of many caves, large and small.

Archaeologists have traditionally demonstrated great physical courage and disregard of danger and discomfort in their field work, and archaeologists on the trail of cave art have been no different. In some caves, they had to crawl through narrow passageways with barely enough room to move. Occasionally they ended up in blind alleys and had to crawl backward all the way to escape. In other cases, they had to wade through small subterranean lakes, cross subterranean rivers, or dive below the surface and swim under water in order to find a chamber where paintings awaited them.

The caves at Altamira, Lascaux, Trois Frères (so named for the three young brothers who discovered it), Niaux, and other sites contain paintings that belong to what is called Franco-Cantabrian art, that is, art of France and the Cantabrian region of Spain. There are special reasons why this art is of such profound interest to us. For one thing, it includes a large number of masterpieces. For another, it portrays realistically animals unknown to later generations. Beyond these virtues, however, is something more. The paintings in the caves were executed apparently from about 15,000 B.C. to about 12,000 B.C. We are not sure of the dates, and we are not sure exactly when scribblers of later centuries added to the paintings on the walls. Nevertheless, they are evidence of an artistic activity that extended over many centuries, not to say millennia, and belong to a tradition later designated as Heroic or Classic. It is constantly astonishing to think that this art was created in a society which was still in the Paleolithic, the Old Stone Age, and that there was at that time no more advanced society anywhere.

The archaeological culture to which Altamira belonged has been designated *Magdalenian* after the name of one of the caves, La Madeleine, in which artifacts and art of a certain type had been found. But what started out as a single culture type was soon subdivided by archaeologists who found that many artifacts and paintings credited to this period differed tremendously from each other. Found at different excavation levels, they were reclassified into culture types from Magdalenian I to Magdalenian VI, the latter being more recent. The entire Magdalenian culture lasted about 5000 years.

The artists of the Magdalenian sites, despite a lack of any written language, had inherited a considerable artistic and cultural tradition. In the Aurignacian culture, which preceded the Magdalenian by about ten thousand years, art had been in a rudimentary stage.

Abbé Breuil, seated with the three brothers who discovered the cave in a chamber of Les Trois Frères. The stalactites, stalagmites, jagged rock protrusions from the cave floor and ceiling, illustrate some of the dangers archaeologists face.

Two bison of the Magdalenian, masterfully carved in clay at Tuc d'Audoubert cave in the French Pyrenees region. The bison to the right is about two feet long, the other slightly smaller.

Aurignacian artists were not accustomed to doing a complete contour of an animal. They left blank spaces between segments of lines, and the pictures were, as a result, vaguer and less effective. They could paint simple silhouettes and little else. On the positive side we must note that they did know how to make deep-grooved engravings, ornamented with occasional finer lines, and that they used color effectively. But this was not the art of heroic dimensions on cave walls.

During the next ten thousand years, artists solved many problems of technique and organized schools which young apprentices could attend to learn the skills involved in painting—the use of graving instruments, the mixing and application of colors, and so on. The large number of engraved stones and implements found at one site in France were apparently practice work, done in the school room —or perhaps we should say school cave.

The art of the Magdalenian cultures reached a peak, or at least a high plateau, sometime between 15,000 B.C. and 10,000 B.C. After that, the precious skills seem to have been lost by the artists of succeeding generations.

Some of the reasons were geological. Earthquakes knocked down the walls of a number of caves and in many cases closed their entrances, so that they were no longer easily accessible to prehistoric man. At the same time, as the ice age drew to a close, the climate changed, and many of the large animals moved north. Prehistoric man counted upon them to provide him not only with food, but with hides, bones, and antlers for making tools and weapons. Where they led he had to follow.

During the past decade, a long held suspicion about Paleolithic man has grown in the minds of many archaeologists to a near certainty. Man was not merely an innocent and accidentally injured bystander during the disappearance of the big-game animals. He helped finish them off. Many of the animals of Europe—the lion, for instance—could adapt to warmer climates than those of Europe after the last ice age. But the lion could not adapt and at the same time defend itself against its human enemies. Man attacked the lion because it was dangerous to him and lived on the same game he did; he killed more and more game animals as his numbers grew.

And large game animals, unlike rats and rabbits, have a long gestation period and do not normally have more than one young at a time. If deer and bison are killed too rapidly, the new generation cannot replenish the stock and the animals eventually become extinct.

As time went on, the emphasis in cave magic paintings very likely shifted from success in the hunt to success in increasing the fertility of the animals upon whom prehistoric man's existence depended. But we have no way of dating any such change.

Every archaeologist has his own theory about why prehistoric man painted in caves, but most of the theories are variations of the basic belief that the caves served as a place of worship. This religious function of the caves has struck not only archaeologists and other scientists, but almost every thoughtful person who has viewed the pictures. The dark chambers, the silence, the animals staring down from the walls and ceilings, and the mysterious abstract figures, as

A horse engraved on a small stone found at La Colombière, France. The numerous engraved lines indicate that this stone served as an artist's practice pad, Magdalenian style.

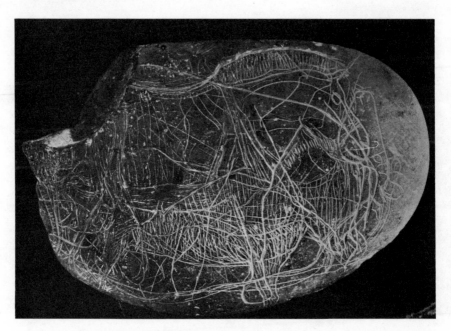

A leaping cow from Lascaux, painted in red with a black head. Note the elegantly curved horns and slender head and neck.

Another leaping cow and two horses, called "Chinese," because of their amazing similarity to horses seen in Chinese art of much later eras. This fresco is from the Axial Gallery at Lascaux.

A close-up of the "Sorcerer." This animal-headed creature may represent a man dressed as a shaman or witch doctor for tribal ceremonies. The position of the picture, both painted and engraved on a high, remote rock, also indicates that it had ritual significance.

A painted horse and several abstract signs on the ceiling of La Pileta, another Spanish cave containing Paleolithic art.

Two of the young explorers of Les Trois Frères, the sister cave to Tuc
d'Audoubert. These two caves comprise a vast labyrinth of chambers, corridors,
and passages, some of them blocked by ancient rockfalls. Several pictures,
outlined in chalk by archaeologists, are visible on the walls. Near the top is
a strange figure, the "Sorcerer."

well as the animal-headed humans grip even the modern viewer with a sense of awe.

It is no wonder that when archaeologists began to track down traditions and folk legends, they learned that some of the caves and the art inside them had indeed been known for many centuries. Medieval priests warned that the caves were the abodes of evil spirits and it was forbidden to approach them. It is possible that medieval folklore about werewolves and vampires may have developed from a vague knowledge of these caves of the devils.

The cave artist did not live in a cave if he could help it. In earlier times, man had inhabited caves because he had no other shelter, and even then he had confined himself to those chambers close to the entrance. Mounds of refuse are not found in the dark inner chambers. As man acquired new skills and tools, he built other shelters and occupied the caves only when weather or enemies threatened.

The Franco-Cantabrian artist may have lived in a tent made of animal skins or in a wooden hut. If he and his assistants could build a wooden scaffold inside a cave, they certainly had the skill to utilize wood for other purposes, in particular for shelter from the rain and wind. But wood did not usually last for centuries, as flint and obsidian did. Bacteria and other microorganisms slowly destroyed both the fibers of wood and the material that cemented the fibers together. Only in rare cases did part of a wooden object survive, occasionally because it was charred, sometimes because it was petrified by the mineral matter in which the flow of water had immersed it.

Fortunately, the Franco-Cantabrian artist's work remained intact long after his home had turned to dust.

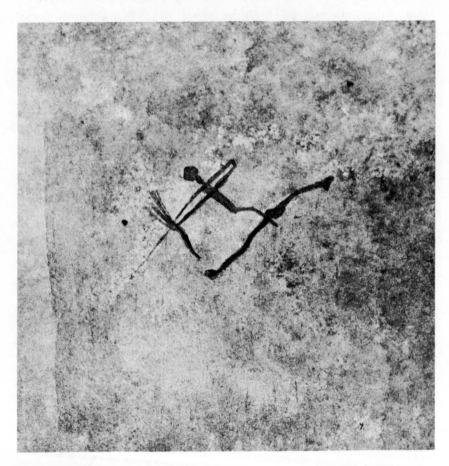

A painted bowman from Cueva de Civil, Albocácer, Spain. This rather crudely drawn painting displays the vitality common to most Spanish-Levantine pictures. This is an archaeologist's copy, made because the original is too badly weathered for clear photographic reproduction.

FIVE

THE SPANISH LEVANT

The Spanish Levant (the Spanish East) is an area of cliffs, crags, and rock shelters. This forbidding terrain, part of the Pyrenees mountains, contains about fifty important sites where rock art has been found, all of it since the beginning of the twentieth century. It was soon recognized as being different from the Franco-Cantabrian art, and in 1907, the Abbé Breuil began the first thorough investigation of it.

Unlike Franco-Cantabrian cave art, most of the Spanish-Levantine art that has been found consists of paintings—engravings being comparatively rare. The paintings are mainly of a single color; red is a favorite, but white and black are also found. The pigments are in general the same as those used by the cave artists, and so was the method of preparation by mixing with blood, honey, grease, or other viscous materials. The paints were applied with brushes made of feathers, fur, hair, or parts of plants, finger paintings being apparently used little or not at all.

The survival of thousands of paintings for so long a time is a fortunate accident, resulting from the combined action of sun, dry air, and water to form a protective coat. This coat may make it difficult to see the paintings and, to bring out the details, archaeologists have sometimes used methods which have harmed the colors as much as centuries of exposure would have done.

The pictures of the Spanish Levant lack the majesty of the great animal paintings of Paleolithic cave art. No magnificent bison seems to charge at the viewer from the depths of a dark chamber, no mammoth raises threatening tusks. The Levantine pictures have a silhouette quality and are much smaller in scale. Some of them were apparently painted to ensure success in hunting, but many tell stories as well, in pictures that are full of life despite their lack of detail. The animals that were then hunted—wild oxen, ibexes, boars—are shown charging back at the hunters. People are now portrayed, revealed in various activities and situations of their daily lives. Some pictures show women dancing. One is of a woman and child, hand in hand. Others are more grim: they show wounded men falling dead from arrows that have penetrated their bodies.

The art reveals a great deal about the way of life. Some women wear long skirts, others loin cloths, the minidresses of that distant day. They also wear bracelets and other ornaments. Warriors are portrayed in their headdresses, which like those of some of the American Indians, seem to be of feathers. Bows and arrows are carefully painted. Some of the men wear long trousers, others loin cloths. In either form of dress they have an exuberant vitality, leaping into the air almost as if taking off for flight.

One picture portrays honey gatherers who have climbed up a rope or heavy vine to reach a hive; one of them holds a container for collecting the honey. They are in a hurry to get everything over with, for they are being attacked by a swarm of angry bees.

The archaeologist extracts all the information he can from such scenes. The container has a handle—and that is significant. It was probably an animal skin, so that most likely the handle was sewn on. But the container may also have been a basket, which would mean that the weaving of twigs had been invented. However, it would require a very close weave indeed to keep honey from seeping

A stag hunt from Mars del Josep, Albocácer. The stags are attempting to escape from the hunter, who races after his prey. The lower animal is badly weathered. A copy of the original rock painting.

Rock carvings from Laxe das Lebres, Poyo, Spain. The male deer, upright to the left, is almost a "mirror" image of the female deer. The disc with nine dots inside is an abstract design, open to many interpretations. Probably late Neolithic period, in Galicia, another Spanish area containing prehistoric rock art.

Four running bowmen, Saltadora, Albocácer. This painting is also a copy of the badly weathered original.

through a basket. Best of all, the container may have been a pot, which would indicate the ability of the honey-gathering people to make pottery.

The human figures are recognizable, although stylized, that is, with some aspects exaggerated and others minimized or omitted altogether. Many figures are extremely long and thin, while others are short and broad. Although most have long thin heads, some have round heads, as in paintings found in Africa. Do these differences in head shape indicate different racial types or are they merely examples of different artistic styles? We do not know, for stylized paintings are difficult to interpret. If archaeologists of the future were to judge our own appearance from the paintings of the famous artist, El Greco, they would conclude that we were all tall and thin. And if they were to judge from some of the paintings of Pablo Picasso, they might conclude that we all had two heads and three eyes.

Some of the men portrayed in the rock paintings have animal heads, as in some of the pictures in the Franco-Cantabrian caves. It seems probable that in both arts, separated by thousands of years, these heads were actually masks, and that the men wearing them were wizards or figures from prehistoric mythology.

All our judgments about Levantine art are uncertain for lack of supporting archaeological data. Relatively few artifacts have been found outdoors near the painted rocks, and it is therefore impossible either to establish the sequence of different paintings in time or to identify objects that appear in the pictures with objects characteristic of different cultures.

Spanish-Levantine rock art has existed for thousands of years. It probably originated near the end of the Paleolithic, in what some archaeologists call the Mesolithic (Middle Stone) Age, and continued into the Neolithic (New Stone) Age.

The relations between Spanish-Levantine and Franco-Cantabrian art are still being studied. In addition, archaeologists have now turned for comparison to the art of southeast Africa. Not only do the roundheads of Levantine art resemble the roundheads of African art; there is also a resemblance between the broad leaping figures. Stone tools, commonly found in Africa, are also found in the Levant region, and the bow used by hunters in the Levantine paintings resembles the prehistoric bow of the Africans.

The evidence strongly suggests that there had been some migration between Africa and the Spanish Levant, although we do not know in which direction. Possibly it was in both directions.

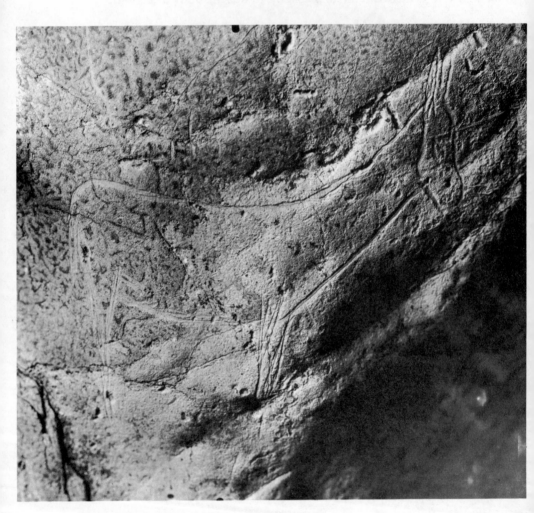

An engraved donkey or mule in Les Trois Frères.

SIX

SCIENCE AND ROCK ART

Chemistry and physics have been contributing to the advance of archaeology from the early part of the nineteenth century. By now they are so important that archaeologists would hardly be able to function without their help. We shall not attempt to describe thoroughly how they have been useful to archaeology in general; but we shall mention some of the ways in which they have contributed to our knowledge of rock art, of the animals depicted in that art, and of the prehistoric artists and their peoples.

The most useful single contribution of physical science to archaeology at present is the carbon 14 method of dating. Students of rock art frequently have been baffled in their efforts to relate the cave paintings to cultures of the past by their ignorance of the dates of the paintings. Whenever dates *are* available, they usually have been obtained by the carbon 14 method.

Carbon 14 is a radioactive element with a half life of about 5770 years—that is, half of it decays in 5770 years, half of what is left decays in the next 5770 years, and so on. It is formed when nitrogen molecules of the air are bombarded by highly energetic particles produced from cosmic rays, the rays that come to us from outer space. These particles transform the atoms of nitrogen 14, which is not radioactive, into atoms of carbon 14. The carbon 14 reacts with the oxygen of the air to form carbon dioxide, and this eventually becomes part of all living animal and plant organisms.

When an organism dies, the carbon 14 in its body decays. The time since the organism died can then be calculated from a knowledge of its carbon 14 and stable carbon contents.

Carbon 14 analyses of charcoal, bone, wood, and other substances that contain carbon have been made, and the method has proved to be extremely useful. Unfortunately, rock art is not usually accompanied by substances that contain carbon, especially in the open air. In addition, the accuracy of carbon 14 dating decreases with age. Although attempts have been made to use it for dating objects as much as fifty thousand years old, the usual limit is about twenty-five thousand years, and perhaps even less.

Other radioisotopes are also used for dating, but they cannot replace the carbon 14 method. They can, however, give us occasionally useful information about some of the rocks among which rock art is found. The isotope potassium 40, found in many rocks, as well as in plants and animals, including ourselves, undergoes slow radioactive decay to the gaseous isotope argon 40. Despite the several billion years half life of the potassium 40, the potassium-argon method, in favorable cases, has been used to date rocks whose ages are measured in merely a few tens of thousands of years. One of the chief sources of error is the escape of argon 40 gas from the rocks.

An entirely different method of dating depends on the finding of obsidian, a hard, glassy volcanic rock that was used for tools and weapons in the different stone ages. Obsidian, over the course of many years, absorbs water vapor from the atmosphere, and forms a thin hydrated skin or *rind*. The thickness of this rind depends on the number of years it has taken to form; a measure of its thickness therefore gives its age.

We can measure thickness much more rapidly and conveniently than we can analyze for carbon 14. Unfortunately, the rate of

A painted horse in Niaux. Note the carefully detailed front hoofs, an unusual touch in Paleolithic art.

hydration of obsidian depends on other things in addition to age, and the method must be used with care. But where it can be used, it gives excellent results.

The "rind" on obsidian is one example of the *patina*, a layer of weathered rock that forms on the surface of flint and obsidian articles alike, as well as on rocks in general. Engraved art can be dated, in a very general way, because the engraving cuts through the old patina and exposes the fresh, unweathered rock below. The time it takes the engraving to acquire a patina of its own gives a minimum age for the engraving.

Obsidian is also used in a quite different way for a quite different purpose—the tracing of prehistoric trade routes. An obsidian object is irradiated with neutrons, particles that have a great deal of energy, but no electric charges. The neutrons convert the numerous impurities, most of them present in tiny amounts, into new, radioactive forms. The pattern of radioactivity thus produced is the equivalent of a birth certificate, for it tells what source the obsidian came from.

Another method of dating, thermoluminescence, makes use of radioactivity in a quite different way. It is used chiefly for pottery,

A sculptured horse in Cap Blanc, France. A detail from a frieze of horses and some bison on the cave wall. The Abbé Breuil identified it as Magdalenian I, the first period of the Magdalenian.

in which so little carbon is present that the carbon 14 method cannot be applied to it.

The clay used for making pottery contains small amounts of radioactive impurities, from uranium and thorium to potassium. As these decay, they emit energetic particles that rip the electrons off the atoms in their path. These displaced electrons, under ordinary circumstances, remain displaced for thousands of years. But if the clay is heated, they can return to their original places, emitting at the same time radiation in the form of light.

When clay is heated in a kiln and converted into pottery, this process of thermoluminescence, or light emission when heated, takes place. When the pottery is cooled, all the electrons are back in their places; in other words, the clock is set back to zero. The more time passes, the more electrons are displaced. If now we deliberately reheat the pottery, the amount of thermoluminescence will depend on the number of years since the clay was fired. A measure of the light emitted gives the age of the pottery. This method is of interest to students of rock art, since pottery is generally agreed to be of neolithic or mesolithic origin, and if found near rock paintings can help to determine the cultures to which the art belonged.

Before considering other dating methods, let us take a brief look at the unexpected ways in which the sciences link up with each other. After the first atomic bombs had been exploded, it dawned on a great many people that strontium 90 produced by atomic fission was getting into plants as well as into the animals that fed on plants, and into us, who feed on both plants and animals. In the human body, strontium 90 is removed from the circulation by the skeleton, where it resides year after year, a possible agent for the production of cancer. The study of strontium 90 in the food chain from plant to man attracted many scientists who, in the next few years, found that there was a fortunate discrimination in animals in favor of calcium in the bones against strontium 90. Consider a plant with a strontium 90 to calcium ratio of 1; the animals who fed on the plant might have a ratio of 0.4, and meat-eating animals that fed on the first animals might have 0.2.

The study of strontium 90 gave impetus to the study of stable strontium, which was found to undergo the same discrimination as

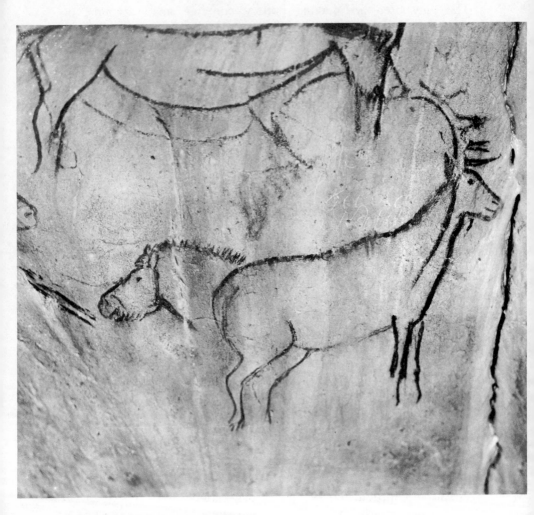

A deer and several horses in Niaux.

strontium 90, compared to calcium. Therefore, an analysis for calcium and strontium in the bones of animals that lived in a given area millions of years ago can distinguish those animals that were vegetable eaters from those that were carnivorous. The method has been little used; other analyses have priority. But it shows how we can assemble fragments of knowledge of the past.

One of the most remarkable methods for dating geological formations depends on a phenomenon discovered only a few years ago —the reversal of earth's magnetic poles. On an average of once every half million years, our planet has reversed its magnetic polarity, the North Pole acquiring the magnetism of the South Pole and vice versa. This has been shown by the investigation of rocks and sediments on the floors of the Atlantic, Pacific, and Antarctic oceans. The sediments came from the rivers of different continents; as they settled down, tiny magnetic particles lined up according to what was the prevailing magnetic polarity. A study of the magnetic properties of the different sediments as well as of the nature of their particles, helps determine the age of the sediments. In this way the ages of several subdivisions of the Pleistocene have been calculated.

Once a dating method is established, it can be linked up with other methods, such as the use of pollen counts. Pollen grains, which contain the male genetic cells of plants, in themselves cannot be used for dating. But their occurrence in different geological layers, or *strata,* shows that the plants from which they came lived during the time when those strata were laid down. Once the dates of the strata are obtained, so are the dates of the pollen in them.

Other methods of dating—such as the counting of tree rings— are well known, and are useful in linking present times with the recent past.

In addition to its use in dating, modern science for years has been taken for granted in the preservation of fragile materials that appear ready to fall apart before the archaeologist can study them. Dry specimens are hydrated with care; wet specimens are dried in such a way as to preserve their structure. Some specimens are embedded in plastic, thus adding the strength of the plastic base to their own. Objects made of corroded metals, such as bronze,

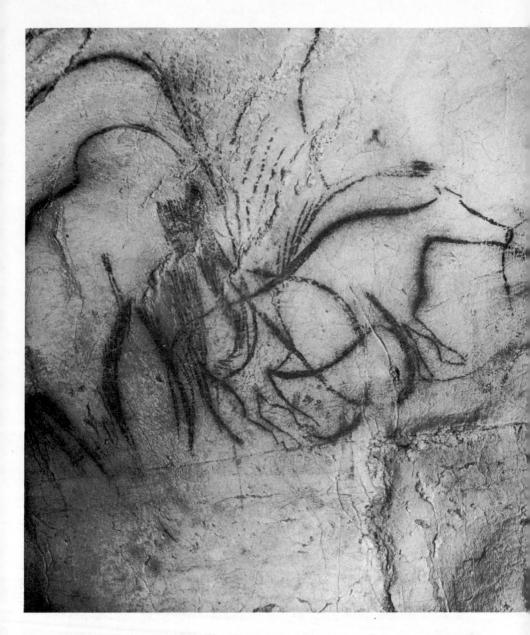

A mammoth, left, and a horse, which is either over or under the mammoth's trunk. The mammoth is not too carefully or realistically drawn, except for the trunk. The cave of Pech Merle in France was first discovered and studied in 1922. In 1949 another section was discovered and named Le Combel. Together, they form a vast connecting link of chambers over a mile long. However, not all the chambers contain art.

Two birds at Les Trois Frères, named "Snow Owls" by archaeologists. The engravings have been chalked for photographic purposes.

may be treated with very small electric currents, thus reversing the effects of corrosion.

Many important questions in archaeology cannot be solved without knowledge of chemical composition. We have seen how chemical analyses for carbon 14, for stable strontium and calcium, and for paleolithic pigments are used to determine dates, sources of mineral supply, and the skills of prehistoric man. In the past, chemists have been limited by their inability to secure large enough samples; naturally, archaeologists did not want to sacrifice a hard-won fossil bone or a sample of paint from an important painting. Moreover, whatever sample the chemist analyzed, he destroyed in the process of analysis.

Many of the modern methods of analysis use very small samples, and some of them are nondestructive; that is, they leave the sample practically unchanged. The neutron activation method already mentioned in connection with obsidian is essentially nondestructive; so is an important method known as X-ray fluorescence.

The X-ray fluorescence method, which requires such equipment as a source of X rays and an X-ray detector, was adapted for use in field archaeology by the University of California at Los Angeles-Israel Archaeological Expedition of 1968. Packed inside suitcases or other convenient carrier cases, its components were transported by bus and train, easily reassembled, and put to work in minutes. In the dryness of the desert and in the humid air of the seacoast, it performed remarkably well and without a breakdown. At the rate of more than an element a minute, it analyzed objects found by the archaeologist, and told him at once if they deserved more careful study in the laboratory.

It is impossible to anticipate in what way archaeology will profit from science next. A few years ago, the use of blood groups was introduced for anthropological purposes. Human blood contains four main types of red blood cells, distinguished as A, B, AB, and O. Each person's blood belongs to one of these types, which are inherited from his father and mother. Blood types were first studied because of their importance in blood transfusions; if blood of the wrong type were transfused into a patient's body, it would cause the cells to clump, and possibly kill the patient instead of helping him.

PLATE 1. Altamira. Two bison from the ceiling of Altamira, painted in red and black. The ceiling is about 60 feet long and 30 feet wide.

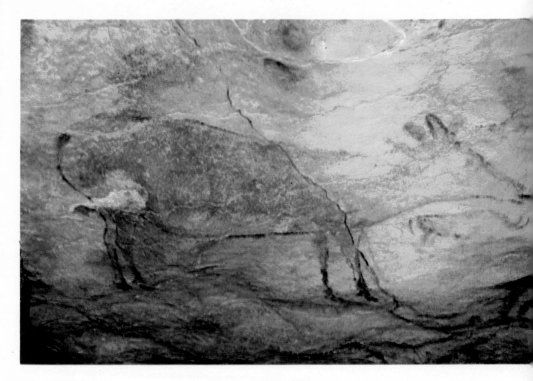

PLATE 2. Altamira. A hind, painted in reddish tones. This animal stands on the left, facing the great mural on the ceiling.

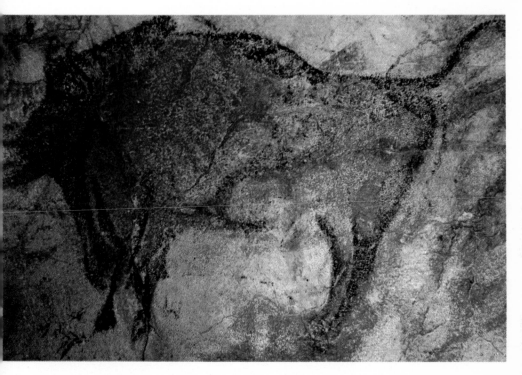

PLATE 3. Altamira. A many-colored bison. The lowering head, the controlled tension of the body, and the tail curled upward combine to suggest that the animal is about to charge.

PLATE 4. Las Monedas. Abstract designs painted in black. Most archaeologists believe that the lines had a symbolic meaning. When the cave was discovered in 1952, coins were found on the floor; hence the name "The Money Cave." Either the cave had been explored by someone in the recent past, or it had been a hide-out for smugglers or other criminals. The art is definitely Upper Paleolithic. Las Monedas is one of a group of caves on Mount Castillo, all of which contain prehistoric, Franco-Cantabrian art.

PLATE 5. El Castillo. An elephant or mammoth. There is some doubt about the correct classification of this beast, which does not have the long-haired woolly coat associated with mammoths. However, as only mammoth skeletons have been found in Paleolithic remains, Professor Leroi-Gourhan is inclined to believe that this, too, is a mammoth. El Castillo, another of the caves on Mount Castillo, was first discovered in 1903, and studied by Abbé Breuil.

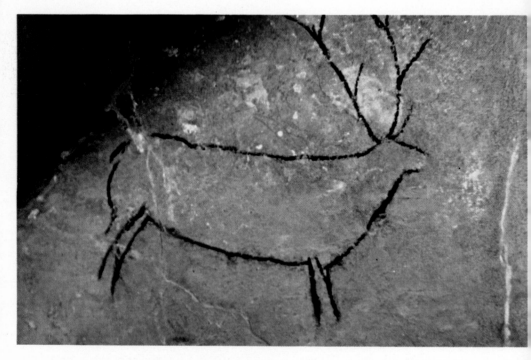

PLATE 6. Las Chimeneas. A painted stag. This cave, also on Mount Castillo, was discovered in 1955. It was named "The Chimneys" because the only means of entrance today are two hollow rock projections that resemble chimneys. The original entrance was sealed off by rock falls many centuries ago.

PLATE 7. Lascaux, France. The wall frieze of the main hall. Although the art here was created during different cultures over a period of thousands of years, the paintings seem to be part of a grand unified design, conceived by a single artist. The animals are constructed on a much larger scale than those at Altamira, the two large white bulls facing each other being over ten feet long. When the cave was discovered, the colors were bright and rich. The cave contains seven chambers with art. The main hall is sometimes called the Rotunda. This fresco includes bulls, deer, horses, and a strange animal known as the "Unicorn." There are several interpretations of the "Unicorn," but the generally accepted one is that it is a mythological creature.

PLATE 8. Lascaux. A rare thing in Paleolithic art, a picture that tells a story, although an unclear one. A man lies dead between a rhinoceros on the left and a wounded bison on the right. A spear has transfixed the bison, and a bird-headed stick or staff is below the man. Some archaeologists believe the bird-head represents the human soul, which takes flight after death. Such symbols are found among present-day primitive peoples. Another interpretation is that the entire picture is symbolic of a ritual of sacrifice or fertility. To reach this chamber, known as the "Well" or "Shaft," one has to descend to another level by way of a ladder. This inaccessibility lends credence to the ritual theory.

The first discoveries about blood typing were followed by the distinction of subtypes, and then by the discovery that to classify a person's blood, the blood itself was not needed. Blood types could be determined in various tissues of the body, and—of great importance to the archaeologist—in samples of bone left by prehistoric man. Thus blood types turned out to be useful in showing the relations between different racial strains, living as well as dead. The different blood types of Eskimo and American Indian groups have helped archaeologists to follow to some extent the spreading of the different racial groups that crossed over from Siberia to Alaska and then turned south.

More unexpected than the use of blood types is the use for purposes of identification of a secretion in the ear commonly known as earwax, more formally called cerumen. Cerumen may be of either two types —wet and sticky, or dry and hard. These types are passed on from parents to children according to the laws of genetics. A study of earwax in the American Indian has confirmed the great probability of his Mongoloid origin. Other studies are now going on to trace the relationship of many different groups in both the Old and the New worlds.

From cosmic rays emitted from distant galaxies millions of years ago to earwax, a sometimes annoying secretion whose function, if any, we do not know, seems like a descent from the sublime to the ridiculous. But both the sublime and the ridiculous are part of our human heritage, and it is fitting that the range of the methods of research should match the range of the subjects they are designed to explore.

A section of the painted ceiling at Lascaux. The height of the ceiling, the narrowness of the passageway, and the utter darkness of the cave give the reader some inkling of the trouble to which Paleolithic artists went to create their works.

SEVEN

PRIMITIVE MATERIALS
AND METHODS

To the modern artist almost everything has become suitable material for expressing his creative feelings—not only the paint and canvas or the marble and bronze of conventional art, but such seemingly unpromising materials as a tin can, a slab of concrete, a piece of wire, a burlap bag, or even an omelet, which can be worked into a type of paste-up art known as collage.

The prehistoric artist was much more limited. His materials consisted of animal tusks, bones, and occasional small pieces of stone as well as rock walls and ceilings, on which he did his carving and paintings. He probably also used slabs of wood and birch bark for painting.

We have no evidence that he expected his art to last very long. In fact, we know that in many cases, he would paint or engrave a picture for temporary use only, and then leave it. His annoying habit—annoying, that is, to archaeologists—of painting one picture over another testifies to his lack of concern for the paintings of other artists.

All the same, he discovered a number of pigments which lasted for a long time and are still being used. He found that the most durable colors were not those he could obtain from plants, but those he could mine from the earth. He ran across some exceptions— charcoal, for instance, a plant product, obtained by the slow heating of wood—but even charcoal black was inferior in coloring power to the black of pyrolusite, an ore of manganese.

If he used colored plant extracts in his rock art, we do not know. After a few years, plant extracts would fade so much that even another artist's eye could not be sure they had been used.

We are on safer ground when we talk of the pigments he did use. He sometimes had a choice of reds—either powdered red chalk or, better, one of the ores known to the geologist as forms of iron oxide, and to painters as varieties of ocher. The ochers gave a range of color from red through brown and yellow, and their coloring power was sometimes so great that they were diluted with white clay to make them go further. Different types of ocher collected in quantities of fifty or a hundred pounds have been found. For use as a pigment, the ocher was ground and then mixed with binding substances, such as animal fat, blood, honey, and perhaps some water.

The prehistoric Franco-Cantabrian artists who used red chalk could certainly have used white chalk as well to give white pigments. Apparently, however, they did not do so. Instead, when they painted a limestone cave wall, they produced a white color simply by leaving an area unpainted.

Franco-Cantabrian painters, like the painters of most other prehistoric groups, seem to have lacked blue or green pigments. Certainly they used no lapis lazuli, a powdered blue mineral, nor any of the blue or green ores of copper. They may have used a blue dye that the tribes of Britain, before the beginning of the Christian era, extracted from a plant called woad and used to paint their bodies. Woad for two thousand years has been regarded as a permanent color. But, like other plant extracts, it was "permanent" for only a few years at most.

Like the artist of today, the prehistoric artist of fifteen thousand years ago applied his pigment in various ways. Sometimes he shaped it into crayons and simply drew on the wall with them. In many cases he dipped his fingers into a pot of pigment and then used his fingers as crayons or brushes. Finger painting was most likely the method he used to produce the patterns of short parallel lines known as *macaroni*.

One method he often utilized was to make incisions or cuts into the rock and then add color to the incisions. A favorite subject, as we have already indicated, was the human hand, his own apparently, as well as that of others. He would lay his hand on the wall, and using it as a stencil, would blow finely powdered pigment around it. He also used this technique to produce a misty effect around an animal, blowing the pigment through a hollow bone tube. Hollow bones with traces of color inside them have been found; the evidence offered by such tubes seems decisive.

Stone palettes and stone mortars and pestles have also been found. However, archaeologists, despite careful searching, have not run across any of the brushes that prehistoric man used, for these were made of materials more perishable than stone—animal bristles and vegetable fibers. But brushes must have been among the most valuable tools he worked with, for many of his paintings required the delicacy of line and sharpness of detail that only brushes could give.

The nature, the size, and the locations of many of the paintings make it clear that the artist was supported by workmen or apprentices who prepared stone lamps, helped in the making of stone tools, mined the pigments and transported them from the mines to the caves, ground paints, and even built scaffolding which enabled the artist to reach the ceiling of a cave. Painting was a social art, practiced for the benefit of prehistoric society and supported by that society.

Several engraved animal-headed men in the cave of Addaura, Sicily. The figure to the left seems to be pointing a spear at the animal below, right. Or is the spear merely a crack in the rock?

EIGHT

ITALIAN ROCK ART

The Addaura cave in Sicily is one of a group of caves scattered over the slopes of Mount Pellagrino. For years it has been used by shepherds to shelter their flocks from cold and rain. As the flocks grew, the shepherds enlarged the cave, digging up the earth floor to a depth of about six feet, and tossing the earth out in front of the cave entrances.

During World War II, the German invaders heard about the caves and used them as arsenals. When the Allied armies drove the Germans back, they in their turn were told about the caves. Upon investigation, they found that the Addaura cave was in fact a storehouse for shells, and rather than undertake the lengthy and possibly risky task of removing them, proceeded to blow them up.

The explosion not only destroyed the shells, but also shattered the layers of calcified rock on the walls and created a tremendous amount of dust, part of which settled on the walls and floor, while the rest floated in and around the cave making it impossible to see into.

In 1947, when peace had once more returned to Sicily, a group of archaeological investigators examined both the cave and the rubbish heap in front of it. In the cave itself they found little of interest, for the air was still full of dust, which was constantly stirred up by the strong winds that blew through the entrance, and the walls were still covered with a thin paste of dust and the water that dripped down upon them. But the excavation heap in front of the cave attracted their attention. It contained both fossils and artifacts which they definitely characterized as Paleolithic. Thanks to the energy of the shepherds, however, it was impossible to tell which fossil or artifact came from which layer, and the scientific value of these earth heaps was very little. The investigators left in considerable disappointment.

For a few more years the caves were neglected. Then they were visited by a wandering hunter who saw engravings upon the walls. The strong winds combined with the unceasing action of the dripping water had finally produced a clean cave.

The archaeologists who now examined the cave found about thirty engraved human and animal figures, which varied in size from five to fifteen inches across. They divided these figures into three groups: the oldest, which were lightly engraved, and two more recent groups, which were more deeply engraved. Not a very large and important haul, it would appear—except for the fact that the human figures are the finest examples of man pictured in Paleolithic art.

As in Paleolithic animal art, the feet are not detailed, nor are the hands. The figures are in outline and the faces in profile. Most of the human figures appear to be wearing bird masks, and there is no facial detail. But the bodies are more natural than the bodies of the few human figures in the great animal paintings, and they give the feeling of motion. The heads, to the extent that the bird masks do not conceal them entirely, appear to be narrow and almost pointed.

The dating of this art as Paleolithic appears correct for several reasons. For one, the patina on the engravings is exactly the same as the patina on the other walls of the cave, both, fortunately, little

A beautiful engraved horse from Levanzo. One of the rare Paleolithic pictures of an animal with head turned frontward.

Painted human figures of primitive design in the Genovese cave on Levanzo.

Two engraved bovides from Levanzo. The lower one's head is turned frontward.

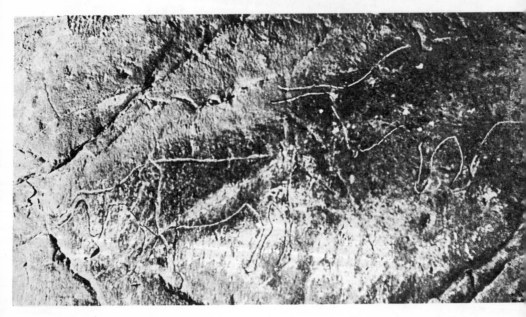

or not at all affected by the great explosions of the German shells. In addition, the bottoms of some pictures were still covered by deposits that could be shown to be Paleolithic.

Not very far from Addaura is the island of Levanzo, off the coast of Sicily. The artists who worked here seem to have had cultural ties with the artists who created the Addauran engravings. Their work was done, however, not in caves but on rocks in the open air. Archaeologists have found here one of the rare examples of an animal pictured with head turned toward the viewer, whereas most prehistoric art shows only the profile. Among the engravings here is a human figure with a bird's head, very much like some of the figures in Addaura.

The great treasure-trove of Italian rock art is in north Italy in the Alps close to the border of Switzerland. Here, in the Camonica Valley, a search has revealed about twenty thousand open air rock carvings, dating from about 2100 B.C. in the Neolithic Age to 16 B.C., when the Camunians, as the inhabitants of the valley are called, were overwhelmed by the growing might of the Roman Empire.

Under Roman rule, and with the impact of the broader and more developed Roman culture, the Camunian culture vanished. Traces of it may still exist in the present-day inhabitants of the valley. But most of our knowledge of the Camunians comes from their two-thousand-year-old gallery of rock drawings.

The Camonican engravings have been known to the peasants of the valley for centuries, but were regarded as signs of witches or of their master, the devil himself, and no one wanted to have anything to do with them. It was not until the early part of the present century that they came to the attention of archaeologists. Studies of the art were few in number and limited in scope until 1956, when a systematic examination and evaluation of the carvings was begun under the leadership of a young archaeologist, Dr. Emmanuel Anati.

The archaeological team headed by Dr. Anati came across thousands of additional engravings. Among their finds were gigantic single rocks on which hundreds of pictures were engraved. Taken as a whole, the twenty thousand engravings are unique in the broadness of subject matter they treat and the wealth of detail they picture.

The Bedolina Rock, Camonica Valley, a prehistoric age equivalent of an urban blueprint. It shows the layout of the ancient fields. Dots inside the boundaries may indicate trees. Huts and human figures at bottom are thought to be later additions.

Two pair of oxen, one leading a wagon, the other a plough. Cemmo, Camonica Valley.

Engraved deer, other animals, and daggers, to right, on an open rock from Cemmo, Camonica Valley.

Although the rock art of Scandinavia, of Africa, and of the Spanish Levant shows us something of the way of life of the artists, the art of the Camonica Valley pictures the houses, the tools, the implements used in farming, and even the domestic animals.

The engravings may lack the artistic quality of rock art found at other sites, but their primitive or naïve styles are familiar to modern eyes. Animals, for instance, are recognizable, although they are not drawn realistically. Some details are exaggerated and others have been minimized or left out.

The very simplicity of the style made it possible for the artist to create his engravings more rapidly and to increase their number and hence their usefulness as a record of their culture and their history. The development of weapons and tools, for instance, is clearly shown in relation to the use that is made of them. Detailed answers are given to puzzles which had previously defied solution. Archaeologists have long known that lake dwellers in Switzerland lived in wooden dwellings over a lake itself. Remains found in the lakes during periods of dryness had given investigators a general idea of their construction, and with a certain amount of guesswork it had been possible to draw a picture of these lake dwellings as they might have been. But in the Camonican rock drawings, for the first time archaeologists saw accurate pictures of these huts, drawn, so to speak, from life.

Anati's archaeological team also investigated the terrain and discovered remains of agricultural terracing by the Camunians. These ancient farmers had cultivated many acres on the lower slopes of their mountains, and the pictures show how. Even maps that date back to the Bronze Age have been found, cut into the rock.

Toward the end of the Camunian culture the artists were painting inscriptions of symbolic figures that may have been intended either as numbers or as ideographs, the first steps toward a form of writing made up of word symbols.

There are many sites in Italy that await archaeological investigation. They hold promise of answering questions that still puzzle scientists about the origin and development of man in Italy.

A mammoth or elephant, chalked by the archaeologist. Note other chalk marks on the rock. The cracks in the rocks have sometimes been interpreted as engraved lines.

NINE

MAKING PICTURES OF PICTURES

How does an archaeologist who specializes in rock art compare cave paintings in Australia with open air pictures in north Sweden half a hemisphere away? As he cannot be in two places at the same time, he needs at least a reproduction of one set of paintings to compare with the actual pictures in the other location. And if he happens to be in the United States at the time he is making the comparison, he needs two sets of reproductions.

The best picture of another picture would appear to be a photo-graph. But photography, in the decades immediately following the discovery of Altamira and its treasures, was still in a primitive stage of development. Cameras were inferior, color reproductions unknown, and the problems of lighting often insoluble. Artificial lighting was then restricted to the use of flash powders, which might have dam-aged the pictures on the wall.

Because of these difficulties, Abbé Breuil and other archaeologists of his generation spent many laborious weeks in the caves, making

Abbé Breuil's copy of mammoths at Font-de-Gaume, France. Before photographic techniques improved, the only reproductions of Franco-Cantabrian art possible were the drawings made by such dedicated scientists.

copies of the paintings and engravings by hand. The discomfort they faced at Altamira was typical and gave them some idea of the discomfort the original prehistoric artist must have felt when they had to paint lying down on the floor or standing on a scaffold.

The copies obtained with so much courage and determination were of great value. But they were not perfect. Either they were flawed in some details or they lacked some of the character of the original. Some of the characteristics of a group of sketches might be due more to the artist archaeologist who copied them than to the prehistoric artist who created the originals. But they were better than the photographs that could be made in that day.

The art and science of photography improved considerably during the twentieth century, however, and archaeologists devised new ways to make the best use of their cameras.

One method was chalking, the outlining of a weathered engraving with chalk to make it more visible. But the very act of chalking requires a decision about what and where to chalk. Is a thin line due to a slight crack in the rock, or was it originally produced by the artist's engraving tools? Each man will chalk what he thinks he sees as part of the total picture, and this may not be what another man might see. Archaeologists often have preconceived notions about the art they are studying, and this method brings their prejudices to the surface.

Another method of copying art is through tracings. Large sheets of specially treated partially transparent paper are attached to the rocks, and the engraved pictures, which can thus be clearly seen,

An archaeologist's copy of a bison from Niaux.

are then chalked on the paper. Plaster or plastic casts of rock surfaces have also been made. But when many engravings are to be copied, these methods are especially tedious and expensive.

In the Sahara, where a group of archaeologists under Dr. Henri Lhote spent many difficult months studying frescoes, weathering had created a shiny finish that made photography almost impossible. The application of kerosene suppressed the shiny glare and brought out details of the pictures well enough for color photographs to be made without damaging the paintings.

One method of photography that can reveal hidden features in rock paintings makes use of infrared light. Ordinary white light contains a variety of colors, ranging from red to violet, the wave length of red light being almost twice as great as that of violet. But beyond the wave lengths that our eyes can detect lie others to which they are blind, such as the infrared. If the visible light is filtered out, the infrared light can create an image on specially sensitized films and can sometimes thus reveal figures that are almost completely invisible in ordinary light. This technique was also used in the Sahara to uncover pictures that had been painted over centuries ago.

In the Camonica Valley of northern Italy, the archaeological group led by Dr. Anati used a modification of these methods to record thousands of engravings scattered over a large number of rocks. First a weak water color was spread thinly over the entire rock surface. The liquid was then wiped away until only a thin film was left in the grooved lines. The color made the lines stand out, considerably improving the photography. Anati was aware, however, that simple photography was not enough. For one thing, all the different parts of a large picture were usually not in focus at the same time, the center often being clear, while the edges were blurred. Therefore, in addition to taking over-all photographs, he also made a mosaic of shots at a medium distance, a number of close-up shots, and tracings. Each type of reproduction added something to the over-all picture.

In Sweden, a photographer who specialized in archaeological pictures found that the engravings, cut into the rock to a depth of only one-tenth of an inch and weathered over the centuries, were

Members of the Leo Frobenius expedition, 1935, copying rock engravings at Ain Safsaf, Sahara Atlas.

Far from the hot, bleak Sahara, young archaeologists trace carvings on an enormous rock in the fertile Camonica Valley, for the Anati expedition.

The bison in Niaux. This picture illustrates the limitations of photographic reproduction. The light, blurred patch is due to a malfunctioning flash bulb.

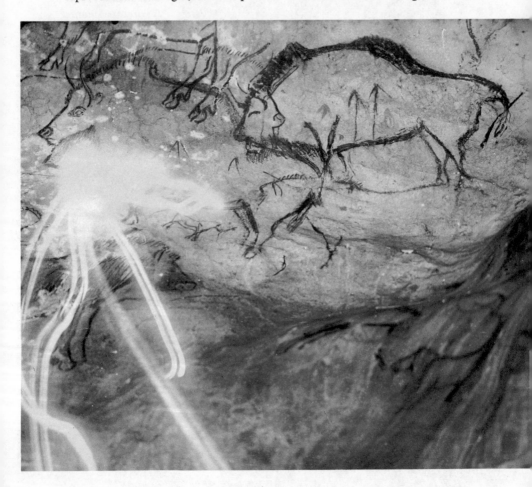

A painted ibex from Niaux. We cannot tell from this picture whether the uneven patches of painting are due to intent of the artist, damage by time, or difficulties of the photographer.

practically invisible in the daytime. At night, however, when a powerful searchlight beam swept over them, the pictures sprang suddenly into clear visibility. Somewhat to the dismay of his archaeological colleagues and the local authorities, the photographer painted the engravings with a thin suspension of lampblack in water. Now the engravings appeared to be outlined with black ink and were easily photographed. The lampblack, to the relief of the worriers, was washed away by the first rain.

In most rock art exposed to the open air, the sun, wind, and rain, and the growth of lichens, mosses, and other plants have done considerable damage. The art in the caves of France and Spain has been more fortunate. Because the caves had been almost completely sealed by such natural catastrophes as landslides and earthquakes, the pictures were preserved for thousands of years. But here, too, paintings and carvings have often been found concealed and damaged by heavy deposits of calcium salts, the results of centuries of water seepage through the rock crevices.

The destructive work of wind and water, unfortunately, has often been helped along by man himself. In several caves, including Lascaux with its magnificent frescoes, man has been an involuntary destroyer. During the past few years it was discovered that the paintings were not only being damaged by the air from outside but also by the carbon dioxide-laden breaths of many visitors. In Lascaux and other caves, all access has been forbidden to the general public until such time as adequate protection for the paintings can be devised.

Some vandalism has been unintentional, perpetrated by quarrying road-building teams, or by farmers, who have moved or blasted rocks without noticing anything special about them.

In the United States and Australia, large numbers of ancient rock art sites have been destroyed by road and dam builders. Sometimes a construction company will delay bulldozing an area where engravings are found, and notify archaeologists of their discoveries. But the number of Indian or Australian aboriginal pictures far exceeds the number of archaeologists, and most of the paintings are destroyed before they can be examined and recorded. In Italy, all discoveries of an archaeological interest must be reported to the authorities, and

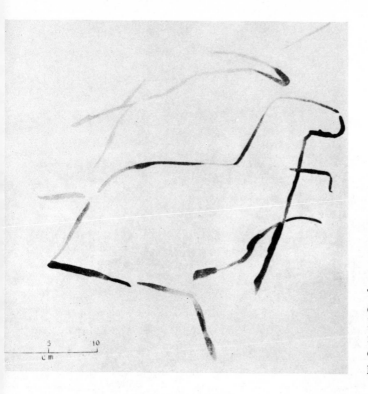

5 10
cm

The archaeologist's drawing of a cave painting from Escoural. The scale underneath gives an idea of the dimensions of the original picture.

work halted until they can be examined and studied. Since such studies can often take years, some builders will simply bulldoze the wonders of the past out of existence without notifying anyone—if they think they can get away with it.

The immediate future holds the promise of a new and superior method of photography for the archaeologist. Scientific advances of the past few years have produced what can be called "pure" light in the form of laser beams. These beams can be used with a new process called holography. In holography, the photographer does not take a direct picture of the object in which he is interested. He photographs, instead, its pattern of light rays. This pattern does not in the least resemble the original object. But it can be used to give a three-dimensional image of the original object, and from this image, pictures can be made at different angles, so that it is possible to reproduce a number of the most effective shots without going back to the object itself, thus saving it from too frequent exposure.

A deeply incised reindeer at Bøla in Nord-Trøndelag, Norway. Late Stone Age Hunters' art.

TEN

SCANDINAVIAN ROCK ART

Prehistoric art is largely concerned with animals, and it is therefore amusing to see how often animals were involved in the discoveries of prehistoric art. In the cave of Altamira, a fox and a dog played leading roles. In Lascaux, Altamira's great rival in magnificence of paintings, it was another dog. In Norway, where the art was not hidden away in caves, but exposed on the surface of great rocks and boulders, the animals involved in two great discoveries were a school of herring and a cow being led home from pasture.

In the early 1900s in Vingen, a small inlet on the west coast of Norway, a group of fishermen, while waiting for their nets to fill with herring, returned to dry land to relax. The inlet was hemmed in by mountains that rose sharply from the sea, and the sun's light struck the rock faces at an angle that brought into view strange figures cut into the rocks. The rocks were old and familiar; the fishermen had been looking at them for years. Now, for the first time, they actually saw them.

A huge elk at Skoger in Vestfold, in the highly stylized "X-ray" art. The lines and circles may represent the elk's inner organs.

Several ships with human figures and wheeled vehicles. These childlike engravings, which have been darkened by the photographer, are symbols, but of what?

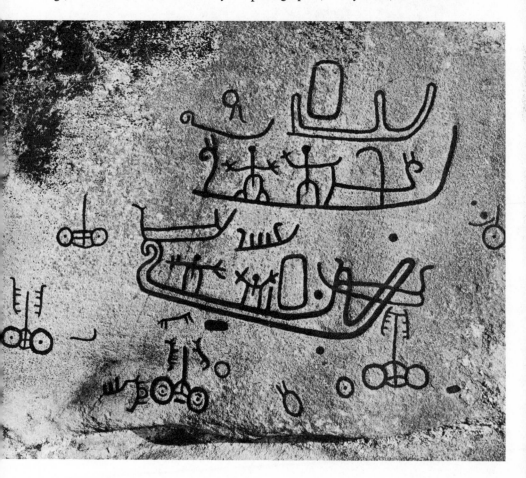

Highly stylized human representations of Fertility, or Farmers' art. The center figure holds tools or weapons. Three figures have only one arm each, due either to weathering or to omission by the artist.

A picture rock at Ingedal in Østfold, Norway. Circles above the ship probably represent the sun and moon.

In a short time the story reached local authorities, who sent qualified investigators to the spot. It soon became clear that these pictures ranked among the greatest collections of prehistoric rock carvings ever found in Scandinavia. Some of them showed large herds of deer. A number consisted of lines and circles that puzzled everyone, although it was soon agreed that these were symbols, perhaps of the sun. Other carvings showed beings that were obviously human, although in stylized form.

In the decades that have passed since then, the number of rock carvings found in and around Vingen increased to about 1500. Most of them, within an area 550 yards long, were examples of the so-called Hunters' art.

Several decades later, while being led home from pasture at a place called Kalnes, a cow accidentally kicked the moss from a large rock, revealing a number of signs and figures that had been carved into the rock. Again the news of the discovery reached archaeologists, who found an important and extensive group of carvings that had been lying here forgotten for countless generations. This art was quite different from that at Vingen. Here, the wild animals of the Hunters' art had been replaced by domesticated animals, by symbols resembling wheels, and by long ships manned by numerous oarsmen. These carvings were classified as Farmers' art or Fertility art.

The icecap that covered Norway and other sub-Arctic areas did not melt until about 6000 B.C., a time when Franco-Cantabrian art had long been dead and its existence forgotten. It was then that human life moved into Norway. Rock art did not appear in the area until about 3000 B.C., although some experts believe that the pictures were done two thousand years earlier. This New Stone Age art came to an end about 1500 B.C., when Norway was entering the Bronze Age.

Hunters' art concentrated above all on animals, indicating that it was used for magic purposes, and human figures played a conspicuously minor role in it. When they did appear, they were small and highly stylized. The fauna of Scandinavian Hunters' art differed considerably from that of the Franco-Cantabrian caves. The carvings depicted few, if any, bison and apparently no mammoths. Instead, there were a great many pictures of reindeer, red deer, elk,

PLATE 9. Lascaux. "Swimming" deer. The arrangement of the antlers, the way
in which the heads on their outstretched necks follow one another, the fact
that the bodies are not visible, all contribute to this interpretation of the deer
as swimming, although the background does not resemble water. This painting
is in the "Nave," a chamber deeper in the cave. Because archaeologists have
all been impressed with the magic or religious purposes, they have given the
various chambers names such as "Nave" or "Apse."

PLATE 10. Pech Merle, France. Two dotted horses, with stenciled hands above them. The techniques used for stenciling hands have not been definitely identified, although it is believed that Paleolithic artists blew the pigment around the hands through hollow bones or tubes filled with pigment. The little finger on the right hand seems abnormally short, and the tip may have been lost through accident or ritual amputation. Red dots are common in this cave, but their meaning is not known.

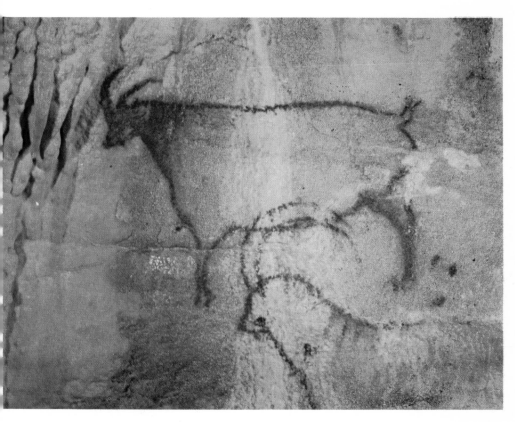

PLATE 11. Cougnac, France. Two ibexes, male and female, presumably mates. When this cave was first explored in 1949, numerous artifacts, such as tools, lamps, and paints were found, as well as a number of animal bones. Professor Leroi-Gourhan and other archaeologists believe that the art here is all from one period.

PLATE 12. Canyon de Chelly, New Mexico. A Basket-Maker painting of hands and several crude human figures. Its age is not known, but is not likely to be more than several hundred years at most. The hands on the upper part of the painting were painted on, probably through smearing the hand with pigment and then pressing the wet hand onto the rock. The hands lower down were stenciled.

PLATE 13. Elephant Cave, Mtoko area, Rhodesia. An elephant hunt. Probably prehistoric, although the date is uncertain. Note the similarity of the human figures to those in Spanish-Levantine and north African rock art.

PLATE 14. Tsisab Gorge, Brandberg, southwest Africa. The "White Lady" of Brandberg is the figure in the center, holding a quiver and arrows in one hand, and a flower or cup in the other. Abbé Breuil saw European, or Mediterranean, facial characteristics in her appearance. The grace of the arms in all the figures does suggest that they are female. However, the "White Lady" carries weapons, probably for war or hunting, which are usually masculine occupations. Considerable mystery surrounds the meaning of this painting.

PLATE 15. Oenpelli, Australia. An X-ray Turtle to the left, a mythical white figure to the right, and smaller figures at bottom, right, give the viewer some idea of the difficulties in dating and identifying the older pictures, which have been partially drawn over.

PLATE 16. Lascaux. These two bison, back to back, charging in opposite directions are among the most powerful representations of Paleolithic art. They are found in the Nave, where the five delicate deer seem to be swimming, and provide a fierce and dramatic contrast.

and a small number of carved bears. In certain areas of Norway, many birds, usually water birds, were depicted, along with fish and whales. Some of the figures were tremendous, one picture of a whale being twenty-seven feet long. Many boats were shown, possibly canoes covered with animal hides.

A number of strange abstract signs occur, along with animals carved in what can be called "X-ray" style. The body of an elk, for example, its outline clearly recognizable, may be covered with mysterious lines and circles. They may have been artists' symbols for the heart, veins, and entrails, or for fertility rites. No one knows for certain.

Although there are many rocks in the areas where Hunters' art has been found, only certain rocks within circumscribed limits have been carved. There must have been strong ritualistic reasons for the choice of specific sites.

The discoveries at Vingen and Kalnes, although important, were not the first. The earliest discovery of Scandinavian rock carvings appears to have been made in 1627 by Peter Alfson, a Swedish teacher. Knowing nothing of prehistoric man, Alfson attributed the rock carvings to the work of medieval masons who had built a church nearby. Two hundred years later, a famous Swedish chemist, Jens Jacob Berzelius, also developed an interest in them and came to the same conclusion. By 1869, however, B. E. Hildebrand, an archaeologist, declared that these carvings, at Bohuslan, Sweden, dated back to the Bronze Age.

Like the pictures at Vingen, they are not in a naturalistic tradition. However, the art of Bohuslan tells us more about the Bronze Age than do all other prehistoric artifacts. The pictures of boats with large numbers of oarsmen reveal that men had learned to build ocean-going ships that liberated them from their own coast lines. The boats were to evolve into the future Viking vessels. Pictures of wheeled vehicles indicate that man had taken a giant step forward, for the wheel enabled him to do many things he had never done before. The domesticated cattle show us that he was now ensured a better supply of food, while the tamed horses and their riders demonstrate that communication between communities was easier, permitting the exchange of objects and ideas. Odd symbolic engravings are seen in both

A Bronze Age carving at Källby, Sweden. This picture, like most of the other Scandinavian illustrations, was darkened with lampblack by the photographer.

Sweden and Norway, including footprints and strange saucerlike depressions carved into the rock. These symbols tell us that the people now had new religious beliefs although they do not tell us what those beliefs were.

The human figures are still very stylized, possibly because of taboos against the accurate reproductions of human images. But scenes of battles indicate that the taboos do not extend to the taking of human lives. Wars between tribes were not uncommon, and the battle scenes display the advances made in weaponry.

The thousands of rock carvings found in widely separated areas all over Scandinavia show great similarities in style. There must have been contact among the artists of different areas, enabling them to exchange ideas and techniques. Great skill was required to be able to tap or chisel deep, precise strokes into a rock, and it is very likely that preliminary sketches served as guides for the artists.

Not all the carvings found have been of the same quality. The later art seems to have been executed more rapidly, and without the care of the Hunters' art.

As most Scandinavian art has been exposed to the harsh climate for centuries, much has been obliterated. Except for slight traces of red paint in the crevices of some pictures, whatever pigments were part of the original carvings have disappeared, and we are left with a tremendous number of pictures of animals, signs, and people, whose meanings and purpose we do not understand.

A montage of tracings from several Siberian sites. The stylized animal resembles Scandinavian X-ray art. The human figure, top left, is also highly
stylized. The pictures are from different prehistoric periods.

ELEVEN

RUSSIAN ROCK ART

Rupestral art has been found in widely separated areas of what is now the Soviet Union, from the White Sea and the Karelian peninsula in the west to the distant Siberian east. In the western regions, especially, the knowledge of rock art goes back to medieval times. It was then regarded, like other European rock art, as the work of demons, not men, and monks of the Orthodox Church exorcised the demons by painting crosses over both the animals and human-looking masked figures.

The medieval knowledge of rock art was forgotten until the nineteenth century, when rock engravings were discovered in the Lake Onega region, near Finland, and reproductions of some of the art were published. But no one showed interest in the pictures until archaeologists and anthropologists, inspired by reports of the art found in the Spanish and French caves, joined to study them early in the twentieth century. In 1909 they published their findings and assigned Russian rock art to the Neolithic Age.

Human and animal figures on open rock in Azerbaijan, near the Black Sea resemble African and Spanish-Levantine art. This photo illustrates some of the difficulties encountered in interpretation. Viewed sideways, the stylized humans look like birds in flight.

Like the closely related Scandinavian art of the late Neolithic and Bronze ages, the Russian pictures are engraved upon open rocks. Many are of ships with carved animal figureheads; others are of animals, both realistic and stylized. The "X-ray" stylized reindeer and horses are fairly common. Among the animal pictures are those of manlike creatures identified as shamans or sorcerers. Other pictures show men on snowshoes, and testify at the same time to the nature of the climate and the ingenuity of the ancient hunters.

In a number of cases, naturalistic animal figures seem to have been engraved over the pictures of ships and magic or religious figures. This is unexpected: the usual pattern in other places is for

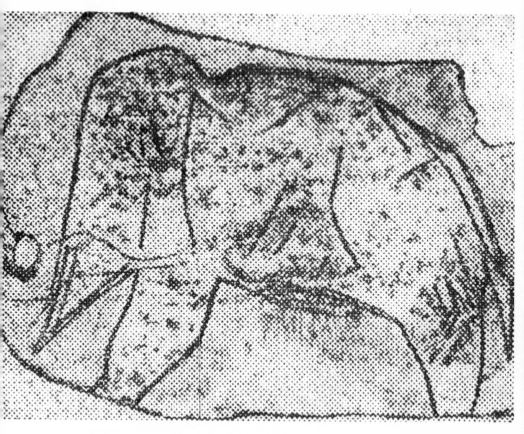

An elephant or mammoth of the Paleolithic, drawn from the original by the archaeologist, at a mineral deposit site near Irkutsk, Siberia.

the naturalistic animals to be underneath. The manner of engraving is also of interest, for the later artists did not use the deep and even chiseled lines created by the northern hunter artists. Instead, they pecked out the stone, as did the North American Indian artists.

The ice age disappeared late from northern Russia, even later than from Scandinavia, and in one sense still exists there, in vast areas of *permafrost,* where the soil below the first few inches or feet is permanently frozen. Moreover, between the different ice ages of the Pleistocene, the Siberian ice melted to form great inland lakes, where it was thought neither hunters nor farmers could live.

During the past few years, however, Soviet archaeologists have made highly important discoveries that have demonstrated the existence of man in Russia about thirty thousand years ago, before the last glaciation. Among the finds are a group of Upper Paleolithic paintings in red. Some are abstract signs. Most of them, however, portray mammoths, rhinoceroses, and horses. These pictures, found in Kapova, a cave in the Ural mountains, exhibit great similarities to the Franco-Cantabrian art. They are located deep within the cave and seem to have had the same ritualistic purpose as the Franco-Cantabrian art. Since these are the only other Paleolithic cave paintings known to exist east of France and Belgium, their importance to the study of man's life, his migrations, and his development cannot be overestimated.

Soviet archaeologists have also excavated the remains of a Cro-Magnon man who had been buried in clothing and ornaments. From the fragments, they were able to reconstruct the style of the outer garments worn in a glacial area over thirty thousand years ago. Another fascinating find was a house built of mammoth bones near the Arctic Circle. The great bones were probably a frame for skin coverings, but this is not certain.

In the same area, excavation revealed artifacts made of obsidian, whose closest source is almost two thousand miles to the south. How did the inhabitants acquire the obsidian? Were they on a trade route or did they themselves make the trek to get it?

Sites containing remains of Mousterian, or Neanderthal, man have also been uncovered, including a cave in which a Neanderthal child was buried.

Discoveries in Siberia suggest, on the basis of carbon 14 analysis, that human occupancy of this forbidding area dates back to more than thirty thousand years ago. This is a much earlier period than had previously been thought. Excavations near the Bering Strait have disclosed a number of artifacts of use value, as well as some of great artistic value.

Since the Soviet Union places a high priority on archaeological studies, and probably has more archaeologists than any other country in the world, further investigation should soon give a more accurate picture of the early wanderers who reached Alaska and led the human invasion of a New World.

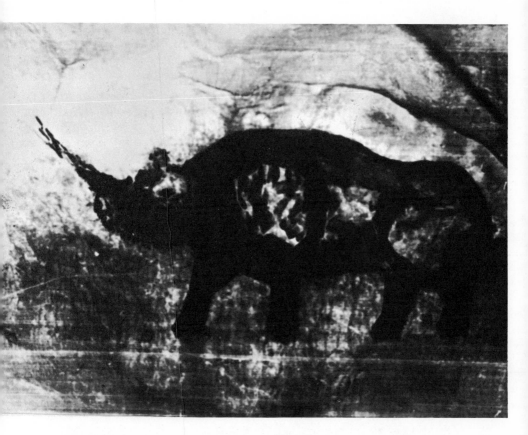

A rhinoceros from the Kapova cave in the Ural mountains, far from the closest Paleolithic art caves in western Europe.

Engraved bear and mountain sheep, with hunters shooting arrows at the bear. The holes in the rock were made by gunshots by vandals.

TWELVE

AMERICAN INDIAN ROCK ART

The first scientific study of native American art was published in 1886 by Colonel Garrick Mallery. Mallery's investigations covered the art created on bone, wood, and animal skins, as well as on rock walls. But publication of the first general study devoted solely to this subject (*Rock Art of the American Indian,* by Campbell Grant), did not come until 1967, almost eighty years later.

Why the long period of neglect? New World rock art had been known for centuries. In 1673 Father Jacques Marquette noticed monsters painted on a cliff in what is now Illinois. Other explorers found similar monsters on rock in other areas of the country. Even the children of the Pilgrim Fathers at sometime before 1680 noticed a rock on the shore near Dighton, Massachusetts, which was covered with incomprehensible designs.

Nor was neglect due to the rarity of this art. In the United States alone, pictures have been found at thousands of sites, and there appear to be thousands more in Canada and Mexico.

One reason for neglect was undoubtedly the low artistic level of many of the paintings and engravings. Native American rock art did not approach the heights of Franco-Cantabrian art and much of it looked like the work of children. Some of it, in fact, was. But many pictures, as is now being recognized, showed talent and great skill.

Then, too, there were comparatively few archaeologists in the United States, and most of them were more interested in the ancient art of the Old World than in that of the New. Since the American Indian was not extinct, there was no stimulus to study their art.

But Indian art deserves study for other reasons. Archaeologists have long regretted the lack of information about the migrations from Asia into the Western Hemisphere, and rock art may yet be of some help in filling the great gaps in their knowledge.

During the million or so years in which man was evolving out of ape man in the Old World, the Western Hemisphere went its own way. The date when man first set foot in this new paradise has

Deeply incised design on a boulder near Ambrose, North Dakota. The engravings were painted over as an aid to photography.

been set at ten thousand years ago, then increased to fifteen thousand years, and increased once more—with a great deal of uncertainty— to about twenty-five thousand years. Some scientists now believe the date to be even earlier. The world was still in the grip of the ice ages of the Pleistocene, not only in Europe and Asia, but also in the North American continent, as a great sheet of ice covered Alaska, Canada, and much of the northern part of the United States.

It has long been known that there was a land bridge between ancient Siberia and Alaska, in the area that is now known as Bering Strait. When the Northern Hemisphere entered its final ice age, the ice sheets locked up vast amounts of water which could no longer pour into the oceans, and, as we have already noted, the sea level dropped. At the same time, the mass of ice that weighed down northern North America depressed the level of the land; to balance this depression, the Bering Strait area rose still farther.

The Bering Strait alternated between dry land and strait, shifting from one to another as the amount of ice increased or decreased. During the periods of dryness, prehistoric Siberians migrated across the land bridge. They came in waves, small or large, depending on the nature of the land bridge, driven by the pressure of hunger or possibly of enemies in Siberia.

In Alaska, in Canada, and in what later became the United States, the existence of millions of large food animals that had never learned to fear man made hunger a thing of the past for the skilled hunters. But as the hunters took their toll the number of large animals decreased, and those that were left learned caution. The invading tribes poured ever southward in their search for favorable territory not occupied by a stronger rival—through Canada, the United States, Mexico, Central America, and South America, almost to the southern-most tip. Relatively small numbers turned off to the east in Canada and the United States.

The immigrants were of many racial strains, and although their descendants have been predominantly Mongoloid, they did not fuse into a single group. The Eskimos, the Indians of the Northwest, the Navajo, the Aztecs, and the Incas all have slightly different physical characteristics.

Most of the American rock art has been found in the West. Part of it consists of naturalistic engravings or paintings of such animals as deer, sheep, fishes, and birds. A mythical thunderbird, which creates thunder by flapping its wings and launches lightning strokes by closing and opening its eyes, is a favorite subject. So are such mythical figures as a plumed serpent and a humpbacked flute player. Symbols abound, and in some of them we can recognize the thing symbolized. Bear tracks, often found, are symbolic of the grizzly bear, whose power the Indians evoked by making him their totem animal, or spiritual watcher.

Engravings far outnumber paintings, which are more vulnerable to the attacks of weather. Whether engraved or painted, most of the pictures are abstract. However, there are men wearing animal masks, as in European rock art, and amazingly enough, there are many pictures of hands. In Monterey County, California, in one of the rather uncommon examples of art in caves, there is a wall covered with hundreds of handprints, with the smaller prints of children below, and the large prints of adults above. It appears that everywhere in the world the power of the human hand in raising man above the level of other animals is recognized.

As in other rock art, we sometimes find pictures engraved over older pictures. In those cases where we can tell which was created first, we have relative dating. However, the dating problems in America are even greater than those in other areas. Where no carbon 14 dates are available, archaeologists must judge by less definite criteria. They may try to guess the age of a picture by the patina on the rocks. But patinas form in different lengths of time, depending on the rock and on the site itself. Sometimes archaeologists attempt to date a painting by measuring the degree of erosion, the wearing away of the rock by wind and rain. Another method—interesting but unfortunately of limited use—depends on measuring the rate of lichen growth over the rock and its pictures. A lichen is not a plant, but a colony of two plants, a fungus and an alga, which grow together in an environment where neither could survive alone. The lichen colony grows at different rates in different places and even on parts of the same rock, and the rate may be as low as a hundredth of an inch a year.

Sometimes the picture helps fix its own date. Two thousand years

A sandstone site in Indian Creek State Park, Utah, containing art of at least three periods. Darker figures at top are assumed oldest, because of the patination. Bear footprints and abstract designs are later. Mountain horsemen and wheel are most recent, since the horse was reintroduced to North America by the white man.

An abstract picture, painted by the Chumash Indians in red, black, white, yellow, and green. There is a slight resemblance, which is almost certainly coincidental, to Australian aboriginal art in this design.

ago, the Indians of Mexico and the American Southwest stopped using the *atlatl,* a device that increased the force with which a spear could be thrown, and substituted in its place the bow and arrow. When we see a pictured atlatl, therefore, we know that the picture is at least two thousand years old. Similarly, as the horse became extinct in North America about eight or ten thousand years ago, the paintings or engravings of horses must be no more than a few hundred years old, dating at most from the time the Spanish invaders again introduced it into North America.

In exceptional cases, even astronomy may supply dates. In two different localities in Arizona are pictures showing a circle and crescent that may represent the moon close to a supernova—a superstar that has suddenly become millions of times brighter than normal. This same supernova was first noted in the Crab Nebula by Chinese as well as European astronomers, and the date was fixed at July 4, 1054. If these drawings really represent the great supernova, we have one of the firmest dates in the history of American Indian rock art.

The most common technique used in engraving was *pecking*—knocking out small chips of stone at a time. Less commonly used was *incising,* or the cutting of continuous lines. No matter how the engravings were made, however, they required little preparation. A skilled man could fashion a flint tool in a fraction of a minute, and if it wore out rapidly, he could throw it away and with little trouble make a new one.

By contrast, the preparation of suitable pigments for paintings was sometimes a slow process. The different forms of ocher used for red and yellow were iron oxides mixed with variable amounts of clay, and they had to be carefully prepared with grease, blood, or some other organic material to bind the particles together. If red ocher was lacking, some of the Indians of British Columbia could prepare it by roasting yellow ocher to drive off as water the small amount of hydrogen that yellow ocher contained. Very few people give the Indians credit for their knowledge of practical chemistry. It was not negligible. Recall, for instance, the Indian method of planting a small fish or two along with corn kernels, long before chemists had learned that the fish supplied the nitrogen needed by the growing corn.

Circular designs, perhaps sun symbols. The site is aptly named Hieroglyphic Pass. Santan Mountains, Arizona.

It would seem that with the American Indians, there should be no difficulty in learning the motive and the meaning of rock pictures, for descendants of the first artists were still painting many years after the white man invaded their land. To some extent this is true. We know that some of the pictures were created by adolescent boys and girls seeking a totem animal, the picture-making being an important part of the ceremonies. We also know that some of the pictures represent a mythology that lasted for centuries. There are clear cases where hunting magic was involved, or agricultural magic, with a call for rain.

Many of the pictures, however, rank as mere doodling. But archaeologists are cautious about calling anything just "doodling," since the Paleolithic tectiforms and macaroni are now being interpreted as symbols of one sort or another.

When it comes to interpretation of complicated abstract or symbolic art, however, the Indians know as little as the white man. Sometimes they have confessed this ignorance. But more often, we suspect, they have indulged the white man by spinning an imaginative cock-and-bull story that would support the white man's theories about their past.

Painted antelopes from Tamrit, Sahara, recorded by Dr. Henri Lhote.

THIRTEEN

AFRICAN ROCK ART

Africa is a large continent, second in size only to Asia, and contains thousands of prehistoric rock pictures. Yet, from the point of view of the specialist in rock art and of the archaeologist in general, it remains largely unexplored.

One or two million years ago, Africa was the home of a man ape, or hominid, and has therefore been regarded by some scientists as the cradle of the human race. About five thousand years ago it was the home of the ancient Egyptians, who developed one of the earliest civilizations. But until only a few decades ago, the hundreds of thousands of years between these two vastly different kinds of human life in the same continent remained an almost complete blank. Very slowly, archaeologists have begun to fill in this blank and to discover stone tools and skeletal remains of intermediate types of men and human cultures.

Most of the known rock art occurs mainly in two widely separated areas, and we shall discuss the two groups separately.

NORTH AFRICA

As far back as 1850, and probably earlier, travelers crossing the Sahara Desert had seen paintings and engravings on outcrops of rock. Although most of these pictures were in rugged areas, off the beaten caravan paths, they were ascribed to Africans who were supposed to have created them for lack of anything better to do during rest stops.

In 1874 an explorer by the name of Rohlfs mentioned these carvings in a book he wrote. More than half a century later, in 1932, Italian scientists who were interested in prehistoric art read the book and acted upon the information it contained by setting out on an expedition to Libya, which was then an Italian colony. They found hundreds of carvings of different artistic periods and apparently of different ages. But the 1930s saw both the invasion of Ethiopia by the Italian Fascist dictator, Benito Mussolini, and the early stages of World War II. Archaeological studies came to a halt.

Some time after the war ended, Italian archaeologists led by Professor P. Graziosi resumed their study of African rock art. In addition, another team of archaeologists and artists led by the French archaeologist, Dr. Henri Lhote, explored the extremely rugged Hoggar mountains. In the Tassili-n-Ajjer massif (a massif is a self-contained mountain which includes at least one peak of its own within a larger mountain range), Dr. Lhote's group discovered, over a period of sixteen months, more than fifteen thousand pictures, many of which they copied, studied, and classified.

We need waste little time wondering about the artists who created their works in the middle of a desert. The fact is that at the time these artists lived, the Sahara was not a desert. While the Northern Hemisphere was struggling under its burden of ice, moisture-laden clouds were deflected south to Africa, and the Sahara region was a green and fertile land.

Scholars have searched the historical records of ancient times, from the clay brick tablets of the Sumerians and Babylonians and the papyri of Egypt to the Bible and the histories of Herodotus, for clues as to when the Sahara became a desert. And geologists

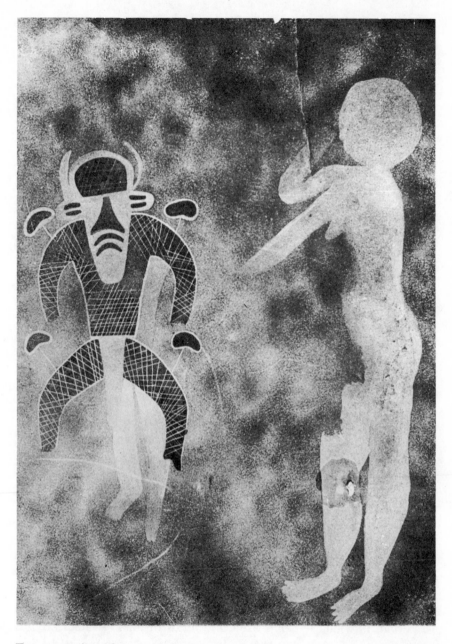

Two mysterious figures of the Round Head period. Note the white figure under the dark masked human. The woman to the right is called White Lady with Round Head. A number of painted human figures in Africa have been considered Caucasian because of the color of the paint used. Whether they were is a matter of dispute. A possibility is that this woman was albino, and therefore thought worth painting.

have explored the Sahara itself, its rocks, its sands, and its few fertile oases to try to follow the desert-making process in detail.

Perhaps the best clues have come from pollen dating. Pollen grains found in excavations have been identified as coming from oaks, cypresses, and olive trees—not one of them suited to desert life. Their ages have been found to range from about 3500 to 3000 B.C., the period just before the entrance of ancient Egypt into world history.

The bones of a now extinct buffalo, the *bubalus,* of lizards, and even of fish testify to the ability of the Sahara to sustain animal and especially human life. The Sahara remained fertile and wet far beyond the end of the last ice age in Europe and into Neolithic times.

The change to a dry desert seems to have taken three or four thousand years and meant disaster not only to the animals that furnished food to man but to man himself. It is very likely that tribes migrated from their native homes in the search for food and water, and that the encounters of different tribes, either peaceful or hostile, led to the rapid development of new skills and the birth of Egyptian civilization.

The pictures themselves portray some of the changes in animal and human life, and make it clear that all regions in the Sahara did not become desert at the same time. The oldest pictures include the bubalus, as well as such large undomesticated animals as the rhinoceros, giraffe, elephant, some of the antelopes, and birds, none of which are desert animals. These were used for food, and the art in which they appear was called by Lhote and others the Bubalus or Hunter period. Some of the engravings are several feet long, while others are miniatures, a carved elephant, for instance, being only seven or eight inches high. Engravings are chiseled or pecked into various types of rocks, from the relatively soft sandstone to the hard granites. In some cases the artist appears to have needed scaffolding, while in others he had to work while lying on his back.

Following the Hunter period, according to Lhote, came the Pastoralist period, in which tethered oxen and herds of domesticated animals are shown with their herdsmen. Paintings now accompany the engravings. This period has been dated, somewhat uncertainly, as extending from about 4000 B.C. to 1200 B.C.—from the prehistory of Egypt well into the history of Egyptian civilization.

Following this came the Horse period, which is comparatively easy

A copy of a rock engraving at Bou Alem, Sahara Atlas. The spheres above the ram and lower animal probably represent the sun; the lines attached to them may be rays or wings. The two vertical animals in the frame very likely had mythological significance. Note the collars around the necks of the three animals; they suggest domestication of livestock, and would place the picture in the Farmers' art culture. Traces of pigment found in the crevices indicate that the pictures had also been painted.

A group of bowmen who seem to be battling over cattle. The drawings of the human figures are crude, but full of life and motion, like Spanish-Levantine art. The original is badly weathered.

to date, as the horse was introduced into the Sahara through Egypt, where it first appeared about 1550 B.C. The pictures show chariots of different types and times. In the Horse period, paintings of the large wild animals of previous periods are absent.

The final period is that of the Camel. This animal was better adapted to life in a desert than the horse, and had become, in the eyes of the artists, the more important beast.

However, the fifteen thousand paintings and engravings at Tassili include many which cannot be classified in any of the four periods. These are called "Round Head" pictures; they portray people in highly symbolic styles, the faces either covered with masks, or without features. Some of the figures are up to sixteen feet high. The name "Round Heads" is a purely descriptive one, for the human heads are all round. Another name given somewhat facetiously to some of these pictures is "Martian" because the human figures seem to have antennae growing out of their heads, as in present-day stereotyped conceptions of what creatures from outer space look like.

Other paintings are noteworthy because they show the figures ornamented and clothed. All these hard to classify pictures are obviously very old, but dating them is not easy, for we have no knowledge of the people who painted them and of the purpose of the artists. Archaeologists have given some of the figures fanciful (and usually unsuitable) names, like the "White Lady" of Inaouanrhat. The people in the pictures have been pronounced by some archaeologists to be white, by others black.

In the pictures at Oran, people are shown in attitudes of prayer. In this area, the extinct bubalus is sometimes accompanied by human figures, whereas in other areas, Bubalus art shows animals only. Most of the later work is painted in many colors. Ochers can be found in the desert, and it is quite possible that other pigments were obtained from neighboring tribes by barter. Some of the pigments were probably moistened with milk, as chemical analysis of the Libyan paintings has shown the presence of casein, a protein found in milk.

In attempts to date these paintings, archaeologists have sifted tons of refuse found on the ground nearby. The garbage of centuries, from the Paleolithic on, has been scattered over a wide area, and

Worship of a bull. The heads of the worshipers are bowed and the hands are clasped in supplication. The bull may have been a symbol of fertility for both livestock and men. This picture at Wadi Sora, Libyan Desert, is probably Farmers' art.

interpretation of the archaeological findings is difficult. Nevertheless, many clues to north African prehistory still await investigation. Many burial mounds of prehistoric man are known, and in a few cases, skeletons have already been uncovered by excavation. The discovery of additional skeletal remains, of animal bones, of implements that can be dated, and of other debris that early man left behind him is almost certain, provided archaeologists are able to raise money for new expeditions. And with greater knowledge of the people who created the rock art of north Africa, the art itself will have more meaning for us.

Copy of a rock engraving at Oued Cheria, Sahara Atlas. The spirals, other abstract signs, as well as animal figures were probably connected with Hunters' magic.

An enormous elephant outlined in dark color and filled in with white pigment. Inside him are elephant and rhinoceros mothers and calves. This picture, one of many in Mtoko cave area, Rhodesia, may be part of some fertility rites.

FOURTEEN

SOUTH AFRICAN ROCK ART

The southern part of Africa is equally rich in rock art, both engraved and painted. Most of the pictures are either in the open or partially sheltered by the overhang of large rock formations, but some have been found in caves. Among them are specimens of prehistoric art equal to the finest known. The subjects include animals, human figures, anthropomorphic beings with human bodies and animal heads, and geometric patterns.

When several distinguished European archaeologists first saw examples of south African art, they discovered in the human representations what they asserted were European physical characteristics. The most famous of these figures is the "White Lady" of Brandberg, so named by the Abbé Breuil. Other viewers have found the human portraits to resemble the pictures of Sumerians, Phoenicians, and even Australian aborigines, while still others fail to see any of these resemblances.

Here, too, as in north Africa, the very large animals, painted or engraved in naturalistic styles, have been assigned to a Hunter period, followed directly by domesticated animals in a Pastoralist period. The third period, however, does not follow the north African pattern; it shows human figures engaged in scenes of mysterious rituals. The fourth period, if there is one, is that of Bushman art. Some rock art specialists believe that there is no Bushman period as such; they consider it probable that all or almost all of the paintings were created by Bushmen in different phases of their prehistoric existence.

The idea that the Bushmen, a small remnant of a once much larger people, could be artists of great native talent and consummate skill has been difficult for some people to swallow. The Bushmen are small not only in numbers but in height as well: their average stature is less than five feet. They resemble the Mongoloids much more than they do the surrounding blacks, and their skin color is more yellow than black.

Driven from their former homes first by the Bantus and later by the white settlers, they fought back as best they could with their most potent weapons, including poisoned darts—and thus acquired a reputation for ferocity. Their artists portrayed some of the battle scenes, against the Bantus, as well as against the whites on horseback, before they were finally driven from the areas where they had lived and painted. Most of them were killed off by their human enemies or by starvation, the few left alive now inhabit the Kalahari Desert, where no other people could survive. Still living in a Stone Age culture, they have been visited and studied by anthropologists, who have found them to be gentle rather than ferocious.

They continued to paint into the latter half of the nineteenth century, and were observed in this activity by white explorers. In their present home in the desert, however, they no longer exhibit their talents as artists. Since they were uprooted and driven from their age-old homes, and their traditional way of life was destroyed, the reasons and techniques for painting and engraving have almost died out.

Some of their myths have survived. Anthropologists have recorded a few of these, and tried to trace their connection with mythical figures in the pictures. However, a verbal tradition changes even as it is handed down from one generation to the next, and over the

The hunters pursuing the small buck are confronted by a charging rhinoceros in this painting at Naukluft, southwest Africa.

centuries, some myths have changed and others have been lost altogether.

The south African engravers of rock art, whoever they were, developed one clever technique for the creation of colored pictures that required no pigment. Taking advantage of the dark patina of the exposed rock surface, they cut down to the lighter color of the unexposed rock below. In this way they carved colored pictures of elephants, zebras, elands, hippopotamuses, rhinoceroses, and a host of other animals. In other areas, these same animals were painted as well as engraved.

Art has also been found in caves of south Africa, in areas where outdoor art apparently came first. Outdoor sites were abandoned when the artists and their people were attacked, and they retreated to caves for greater safety.

In contrast to the pictures on open rock, which were usually engraved, the pictures inside the caves were painted. This may have represented a deliberate choice by the artists of different techniques for the two locations. It is possible, however, that the artists also painted outdoors, and that these paintings have been destroyed by weathering.

The human figures shown are generally in motion, hunting, dancing, running, and using their spears and arrows against animals and human enemies. In some paintings, the artists pictured their own daily lives. Scenes represent families at rest, with gourds, baskets, skin bags, and other family possessions around them.

The active figures in these paintings show some of the same quality of movement as paintings of the Spanish Levant, which have been ascribed to the Neolithic or Bronze ages. But there is no direct evidence of the intermingling of people from these widely separated

Half of a tremendous fresco in a cave in Mtoko area, Southern Rhodesia. The animals are masterfully painted in naturalistic style, but there are also abstract signs, known as "formlings," and human figures, some of whom wear animal masks. Other not quite human figures may be mythological creatures. Several prehistoric styles occur here, indicating use of the cave for very long periods of time.

areas and this similarity in style may be pure coincidence.

Among the mythological creatures depicted are human figures with animal heads, quite different in style and execution from the anthropomorphic creatures of European art. Also to be found are figures that are animal in the upper part of the body, while the lower part displays human characteristics. Parallels and contrasts can be found in ancient European, Egyptian, and Babylonian mythologies. Abstract paintings known as "formlings" have also been seen in the caves.

Unfortunately, although excavations in some of the caves have uncovered microliths, small Stone Age implements, and shards of pottery, these have done little to solve the dating problem.

Some archaeologists believe that the most ancient rock art yet found in south Africa is no more than a few thousand years old.

A procession of warriors or hunters. This impressive composition at Sassa, Southern Rhodesia, resembles some of the compositions of Scandinavian hunters. (See page 86)

A rock carving of concentric circle design at Port Hedland, northwest Australia. Compare with spiral from Sahara. (See page 113)

FIFTEEN

AUSTRALIAN ROCK ART

Australia is a small continent, somewhat less in area than the United States, and much of it is barren desert and wasteland. Yet, at the time the first white man's colony was founded in 1788, it supported a population of about three hundred thousand people. These aborigines, as they were called by the white man, were still in the Paleolithic Age, and they seemed, to the English convicts who comprised the first boatload of settlers, little more than savage animals. They were, in fact, treated as animals, and both on Australia itself and the island of Tasmania, to the south, they were hunted down to supply food for dogs. In Tasmania, the aborigines were exterminated completely.

These so-called animals, who in the tropical climate of most of their continent wore no clothes, had, however, a complicated social organization which later on was greatly to impress the anthropologists who studied them. Moreover, they had a great artistic tradition, and the rocks of the barren land are covered with thousands of paintings and engravings whose history stretches far back into the mists of Australian antiquity.

Australian painting has considerable variety, and shows some fascinating resemblances to rock art on other continents—to the slender stylized figures of African art, for one, and to the so-called "X-ray" art of Neolithic or Bronze Age Russia and Scandinavia for another. Strangely, enough, the Australian art, produced by a more primitive people, is more sophisticated and detailed.

Like the American continents, Australia had no human or near human inhabitants until about twenty thousand years ago. It was the last great ice age of the Pleistocene that finally brought man to Australia. When the billions of tons of water locked up in the great ice sheets of the Northern Hemisphere lowered the sea level, the results were felt all over the world. In the region of southeast Asia and Australia, what had been shallow ocean beds now became dry land. Only the deeper parts of the sea remained under water.

It now became possible to reach Australia from southeast Asia by traveling to a large extent over dry land, sailing or paddling over relatively small distances. It is very likely that New Guinea was the last stop for the large canoes or sailing vessels that these early men used, and that New Guinea was connected for a while, by means of a land bridge, to Australia itself.

But this long trek over land and sea remained open only for a short time, historically speaking—at the most a few thousand years. When the ice sheets began to melt, the sea level rose, and the first settlers of Australia soon found themselves separated from other human beings.

They were not altogether alone. Australia had been isolated from other continental land masses for millions of years. One consequence was the existence in Australia of animals to be found nowhere else on earth. European zoologists who were first told of the duck-billed platypus, an Australian mammal that lays eggs, thought they were being hoaxed. But Australia was inhabited by a number of animals —the kangaroo, the wombat, the koala, and the emu—that were almost equally strange.

The original Australians and their descendants adapted well to the new physical environment and its new kinds of plants and animals. The long droughts created new desert areas from one year to the next, while the scattered rains temporarily transformed seeming

Stenciled hands and abstract designs on cliff walls at Carnarvon National Park, Australia. The crescent-shaped designs represent boomerangs.

A group of evil Mamandi spirits. Note the feet and hands. Part of a larger frieze, painted in red at Inagurdurwil, Australia.

desert to green pastures. The irregular rainfall made it impossible to grow crops in the same area every year. Moreover, none of the strange animals they encountered were suitable for domestication on a large scale. The Australians therefore remained fishers and hunters, and followed the game on land and sea.

They learned to live in an environment so harsh that no modern European could have endured it. They did not depend solely on game animals. They could dig food out of the ground—large grubs and honey-laden ants were favorites—and they could identify and follow rain clouds to obtain the life-giving water that the spirits in the sky sent down to them.

Their daily activities as well as their spiritual beliefs are reflected in their paintings and engravings on open rocks as well as in caves. Unlike the European cave art, which was created deep within the caves, Australian paintings are found near the entrances of shallow caves, or in rock shelters. In thousands of pictures the aborigines can be seen dancing, fighting, and hunting. Like prehistoric artists everywhere else in the world they made stenciled paintings of hands, as well as of feet. And they painted the spirits that they believed were all around them.

Among these were the Wandjina, giants who in some pictures were fifteen feet tall. The Wandjina were humanoid, but lacked mouths, and communicated in ways that ordinary men could not understand. Other important spirits were the Lightning Brothers, whose pictures have been found in caves, supposedly painted by the brothers themselves. Among the most mysterious of the spirits were the Mimi, tall, shy, and extremely thin. There were wicked as well as good Mimi characters. When human beings came too close for comfort, the Mimi simply walked through openings in the rock walls, which closed in behind them. The Mimi pictures bear interesting resemblances to both south African and Spanish-Levantine rock art, and are so old that they are attributed to Mimi, rather than human artists.

The age of the Australian rock pictures is just as uncertain as the age of rock paintings on the other continents. There has been very little dating by carbon 14, and archaeologists have been forced to rely on other ways of estimating age. They study the patina on the rocks; they measure the amounts of debris covering fallen painted

A group of running women. A cave painting near Oenpelli. The first two figures are badly weathered. Note the drawings on the wall below them.

A wicked Mimi, called Adungun, being pursued by an aborigine. The Mimi's stomach is full of human victims he has eaten. The myth tells us that he died when he was speared so often that his stomach fell out, and he thus lost the strength which the engulfed figures gave him. A cave painting at Oenpelli.

rocks, and they compare fossils of extinct animals with pictures of those animals. One clue is an ocher mine, which has apparently been excavated for the pigment for many thousand years. At least a few of the paintings studied should be thousands of years old. But which ones?

Australian aboriginal art is the only prehistoric art that remains alive. Because of this we know some of the reasons for it, and can, perhaps, even draw certain analogies with the long dead arts of long dead peoples.

Some pictures are painted for ceremonial purposes, for tribal rituals. During such rituals, the aborigines also decorate their bodies with painted designs. Other pictures serve to keep the mythology and customs alive, and still others are meant to ensure success in the struggles against nature or against an enemy. In addition to all other reasons, the artist frequently paints for the joy of painting.

The aboriginal inhabitants of Australia differed slightly in different parts of the continent in features, color, size, and culture. Naturally, there were also differences in art, involving choice of subject, style of painting or engraving, and such technical matters as the number of paints used. Many paintings are in a single color, usually the reliable red of ocher. But other pigments, like the black manganese ore known to the Franco-Cantabrian artists, were used, and in some caves, paintings have been found in nine colors.

Some of the pictures have been recognized as very old, dating from the prehistoric period known as Mudukian, when muduks, or bone spears, were used. A few pictures are so old that the aborigines themselves have forgotten their existence and are ignorant of their meanings.

Among the most skillfully created pictures are geometric patterns. These have been transmitted through the generations, sometimes improved by modern aboriginal painters, and adopted by European-Australian artists for commercial use. Similar abstract designs have been recently found on engraved rocks in Tasmania.

The Australian aborigines have been of particular interest to anthropologists because their beliefs are based on *totemism,* a system of religious and social organization in which each clan is related to a *totem,* that is, to a plant or animal which is a kind of minor god

X-ray paintings, chiefly of various fish, in red and yellow, at Oenpelli.

concerned with the welfare of the clan. Eskimos and American Indians also believed in totems, and one may speculate whether the probable common origin of these people in Asia can account for the similarity in their beliefs.

The totem plants and animals play a large part in aboriginal art. The painting or engraving of a picture was often part of a ceremony to ensure good hunting or to bring rain. The ceremony might be conducted by a small group of men or even by a single hunter. Under such circumstances, it would be too much to expect every artist to be a good one, or every painting to be a near masterpiece. We should expect, instead, to find thousands of paintings, good and bad, produced by centuries of ceremonials. And this is what we find.

Australian artists painted pictures that illustrate astronomical myths, not unlike those of the Greeks, as well as others with unexpectedly biblical overtones. A picture of a whale with a human being inside inevitably reminds us of Jonah and the whale. But there is no evidence that the Australian aborigines ever heard of the prehistoric European-Asian myth on which the story of Jonah is based.

Other legends seem to parallel European mythology. The legend about the ferrying of dead souls across the river of death, for instance, is very similar to the Greek myth of Charon and the river Styx.

As in every other place where rock art has been found, a great deal has been destroyed by weather, rock falls, and modern man's activities. With the expansion of European settlements and the building of roads, dams, and houses, many invaluable paintings, as well as artifacts that could help in dating them have been lost.

SIXTEEN

PARALLELS THAT MAY MEET

Anthropologists frequently make use of a method they distrust—the method of *ethnographic parallels,* or as some call it, of *ethnographic analogy.* Ethnography is the study and classification of the cultural and racial groups of mankind. In using the ethnographic parallel method, scientists compare two races or cultures and attempt, from the known behavior of one group, to learn something about the behavior of the other. To take a very simple example, if a peculiarly shaped flint is found in one culture where it is used for scraping hides, the anthropologist may deduce that a similar flint found a thousand miles away is used for the same purpose.

It may turn out, however, that the second group does not hunt, has no animal skins, and uses its peculiar flint for a different purpose, such as cutting through hard wood or rock. It is such pitfalls that make the anthropologist wary of the method of ethnographic parallels.

And yet the archaeologist who studies ancient man has little choice in the matter. How else can he try to enter the minds of men who are long dead? He tries first to understand the thinking of men in Stone Age cultures who have survived into the present—the American Indian, the Australian aborigine, certain Polynesian tribes, to take several notable examples. And then he assumes—knowing that his assumption may be completely mistaken—that in similar situations the ancient artists of Altamira and Lascaux thought the same way.

This method of reasoning involves other assumptions as well. He assumes that the thousands of years between ancient Paleolithic man and present-day Stone Age man have created no great changes of a social or psychological nature. He may also assume that the culture of, say the American Indian, was not affected by the landing of the first white man on the American continent. Or he may assume the converse,. that the Indian way of life was totally altered by the tools, weapons, and animals introduced by the white man. And finally, he assumes that his own ways of thinking have enough in common with the thinking of such people as the Australian aborigine to permit him and the aborigine to understand each other, and to bridge the gap between an urban, industrialized civilization, and a Hunters' culture.

The aborigine may interpret a question in a way that a European does not expect; he may give an answer that means something quite different to the questioner from what it means to him. And to make matters worse, he may volunteer answers that he knows are not true, either because he would like to please the white man and give him what he expects, or because he is keeping secrets he does not want the white man to know.

In any case, whenever the archaeologist is comparing a phase of one culture with its parallel in the other, he is also comparing them both with his own culture. And when he decides to avoid any dependence on ethnographic parallels, he cannot help assuming that some parallel exists between the culture he is studying and his own culture.

Modern man's culture changes somewhat from year to year, and strikingly from one century to the next. One method recently proposed for the interpretation of Franco-Cantabrian art depends on the acceptance of an elaborate symbolism, in which the thousands of animals painted in the various caves had symbolic sexual significance. This theory leans heavily for support on the theories of the unconscious. It would have been impossible for scientists to conceive a hundred years ago, before Sigmund Freud invented psychoanalysis.

In some respects, however, there may be valid parallels between ancient and modern man.

Religious holidays have survived for millennia, beginning as pagan rites long before biblical times, and undergoing many changes to become part of respectable modern ceremonials. Superstitions about numbers still exist today, some of them not greatly changed from the superstitions of prehistoric man. Similar beliefs persist in the power of astrology, and the bad luck associated with black cats and other animals.

Prehistoric man had feelings of awe about mountains, for spirits lived there. That may be one reason why Franco-Cantabrian artists created their work in mountain caves. Even modern man has been impressed by the flashes of lightning and the ear-shattering roars of thunder around the peak of a mountain during a thunderstorm. Greek mythology saw in the thunder the fury of the chief god, Zeus, who hurled thunderbolts at his enemies. Zeus, like the other gods, lived on Mount Olympus. The Bible placed God on Mount Sinai, where Moses received the Ten Commandments.

When Sir Edmund Hillary was asked why he had climbed Mount Everest, about which the Himalayan people have their own spirit myths, he replied, "Because it was there." His answer expressed only one of many reasons. If ethnographic parallels are valid about mountain climbing, he might have said, "Because the gods are there." It would have been a reason perfectly acceptable to our prehistoric ancestors.

SEVENTEEN

IN CONCLUSION

We have traversed the world in our search for rock art and a greater understanding of its creators. With the mass of information gathered during the past century, can we give better answers to the questions we first asked about the Paleolithic artists? Do we now know why they painted?

Our answers may be more detailed, but they are not necessarily better. In the mid-nineteenth century, two famous archaeologists, Lartet and Christy, conceived the idea that prehistoric man painted for no less a reason than his love of beauty. They believed that the first artist could indulge his aesthetic tastes because he lived in a world where game was so abundant that he could provide for his food supply in a fraction of his working day, or even live on the game killed by others.

This was the first of a number of theories that have since been lumped together as "art for art's sake." The theories did not long survive in their original forms. When the Australian aborigines were studied, their lives were found to be difficult ones in a generally hostile environment. However, as we have seen, they still enjoyed painting—sometimes for painting's own sake, at other times for more serious purposes. Nor did the cave paintings of the Paleolithic fit into any of the "art for art's sake" theories. Artists may paint to satisfy their sense of beauty, but they usually prefer to have their works seen, admired, and supported by the noncreative public. There appeared to be no good reason why the Paleolithic artists should express their love of beauty in the depths of caves.

The dominant theory today appears to be that of sympathetic magic. By drawing food animals and showing some of them pierced by spears or arrows, Paleolithic man tried to ensure luck in hunting. And by drawing pregnant animals, he tried to help the real animals in the woods and fields give birth to young, thus ensuring a continuing supply of game.

It is likely that the more gifted members of the tribe would be given the task of drawing or painting these magic figures. The better the reproduction, the greater the identification with the animal itself, and the better the magic.

The theory of sympathetic magic, or some variation of it is not accepted by all archaeologists. One prominent dissenter, Professor André Leroi-Gourhan, has proposed a completely different explanation. On the basis of a long and detailed study of Paleolithic art in sixty-five caves, he thought that he could best explain the nature of the paintings by a theory of sexual symbolism. All the animals that Paleolithic man painted could be regarded as symbolic of male and female principles. The horse was the chief symbol of the male principle and the bison of the female.

Professor Leroi-Gourhan's theory distinguished between the meaning of a symbol painted in the depths of a cave, and the same symbol painted near the entrance. He grouped together, as part of a single scene, paintings of different animals that other archaeologists had considered as being unrelated. And he gave a new interpretation of the so-called tectiforms, the little geometrical forms that had intrigued many investigators before him.

Some archaeologists had regarded the tectiforms as rather meaningless doodles. One small form had been thought by some to resemble a hut, by others to resemble a trap. Professor Leroi-Gourhan considered all tectiforms to be secondary sexual symbols.

In the attempt to prove the correctness of one theory or another, archaeologists have argued about the details of every drawing, of every dotted line. What one sees as a shaman, a primitive sorcerer wearing an animal mask, another regards as a hunter who wears the mask as a disguise to deceive the animals he is hunting; a third regards the sorcerer figure as merely a clumsy drawing of a man or animal done by an unskilled artist.

One man sees the sagging bellies of many animals as indications of pregnancy; another regards the sagging as an unimportant detail of no significance; and still another, a painter himself, considers the sagging evidence for his theory that the Paleolithic artist, when he could, used dead animals as models. This provocative theory has not been accepted for a variety of reasons, partly because the physical difficulties involved in dragging a dead mammoth, or even a bison, into the depths of a cave would have been almost insurmountable.

Sometimes archaeologists create their own difficulties. Several of them were surprised to find a bird engraved on the ceiling of the cave at Rouffignac. But they had been looking at the picture upside down. Seen from another position, it turned out to be a rhinoceros.

Some archaeologists have regarded the rows of red dots seen coming from an animal as symbolic of the spear used to attack it. Others have regarded the red dots as streams of blood. A third group—and there are always at least three sides to every question discussed here—finds the red dots unimportant. Perhaps they were added to the picture by a later artist, or perhaps they were painted by an earlier artist, and the painter simply ignored them and painted his animals over and around them anyway.

It is impossible in this limited space to discuss the many disagreements about the meanings of painted hands, feet, lines, and circles, which have been variously classified as symbols of the sun, the moon, or male and female principles. The geological formations of the caves are another source of dissension. Were the remote chambers where so much art has been found, as remote, as far removed from the entrances in Paleolithic times, or have the caves themselves undergone changes due to earthquakes which may have closed up some entrances and opened others?

Sometimes the archaeologist quarrels with the prehistoric artist himself. A woolly rhinoceros painted on the walls of the cave at Font-de-Gaume was criticized because the artist had painted the shape and carriage of the tail incorrectly. Later, when a woolly rhinoceros was dug up almost perfectly preserved at Starunia, in Poland, the tail was found to be constructed as the Paleolithic artist, and not the modern archaeologist or zoologist, had pictured it.

We know very little about Paleolithic man of ten to thirty thousand years ago, and individuals must have varied then as they do now, but one thing we can be sure of: as a hunter he had a sharp eye for the details of animal appearance. To him these were not academic matters but a question of life or death. An archaeologist who mistook a rhinoceros tail for the twig of a tree would have a temporary red face. A Paleolithic man who made the same mistake might not live long enough to make another. Moreover, in addition to being a sharp observer of details, he also had a good memory. Living before writing was invented, he had nothing but his own mind to keep him from forgetting things.

We have learned so much about a few groups of prehistoric men that we tend to forget how much of vital importance we do not know. We know nothing of his speech, and it is difficult to imagine how we can possibly learn anything about it. At what stage, before or after the earliest manlike creatures had begun to evolve, did human speech begin? The first collection of sounds that deserved to be called human language must have given a considerable advantage to the group that used it and may have led to its triumph over other manlike creatures.

With speech must have come rhythmic chants and songs with or without words. It is difficult to believe that magic ceremonies of any kind would be unaccompanied by drumbeats or impressive ritual chants.

If we judge by ethnographic parallels, we must assume that prehistoric man used hallucinogenic drugs. Not as deadly as LSD and other modern chemicals, they were undoubtedly chewed or drunk by witch doctors, wizards, shamans, and medicine men to put themselves and possibly other members of the tribe into a trancelike state and to create vivid hallucinations. Such drugs can be obtained in great variety from plants all over the world.

The archaeologist is interested in every detail of prehistoric man's daily life, and it is pertinent to ask why. Although we are still in disagreement about why the prehistoric artist painted, it should be easier to learn why the archaeologist delves into the past. What does he expect to get out of it? After all, the paintings cannot be removed from their rocky sites to ornament a palace or museum as treasures of gold, silver, or marble can.

There are many personal reasons, differing from one archaeologist to another. In general, it would be true to say that he digs into the past chiefly because he is intensely interested in it. He follows the advice of the philosopher Socrates to "Know thyself," and of the poet, Alexander Pope, that "The proper study of mankind is man."

As a practical man, as well as occasional poet and sometime philosopher, he studies man's past in order to know the present better and to predict the future. Most of us would be very happy to receive the slightest hints as to where *Homo sapiens* is going these difficult and exciting days. A knowledge of the past thirty thousand years may possibly give us one or two of those hints.

Pity the poor archaeologist of the future who attempts to find an ethnographic parallel between this photograph and that on page viii. Although the hand looms large in both, we know that this picture was posed in a studio for the purpose of selling synthetic fabrics, while the other was painted on rock several thousand years ago, probably for religious or magical reasons. The archaeologist of the future may believe, however, that fashion also had its worshipers in the twentieth century.

touch ™
Caprolan® nylon
It feels different because it is.

Leo Narducci: Swirls and folds of beautiful silken Caprolan TOUCH nylon draped, as only TOUCH can, into one magnificent pajama, deep-buttoned at wrists and midriff. In colored-pattern brilliance by Soptra. Sizes 6-16. Retail at about $125. Also in earth-and-sunrise colors. At finest stores.
Photographed at Pirate's Cove, Paradise Island, Nassau in The Bahamas

GLOSSARY

ANTHROPOLOGY: the science of man. It includes all aspects of man's life, his origins, physical and social evolution, and culture. Derived from the Greek, *Anthropos*—man, and *Logos*—speech or discourse.

ARCHAEOLOGY: the science of man's past, both prehistoric and historic, through study of what he left behind. From the Greek, *Archaos*—ancient, and *Logos*—speech or discourse.

ARTIFACT: any object made by man, or changed by man for his use, from a chipped stone to a space ship. From the Latin, *Ars*—art, and *Factus*—made.

AURIGNACIAN, *see Culture*

BRONZE AGE, *see Culture*

CULTURE: the way of life of any group of people, including its tools, industries, religion, etc. From the Latin, *Cultura*—cultivation, tending, or tilling.

  AURIGNACIAN: a prehistoric culture, so named for Aurignac, France, where evidence of its existence was first found. Existed from about 35,000 B.C. to about 20,000 B.C.

  BRONZE AGE: the stage of human development following the Neolithic, or New Stone Age, so named because implements and weapons were made of bronze. It lasted for various lengths of time in different places, but is generally believed to have begun around 3500 B.C. in the Mediterranean area. The first written languages arose in this age.

  MAGDALENIAN: a culture of the Upper Paleolithic, which lasted for about ten thousand years in France, Spain, and parts of central Europe. The era of the heroic cave art of Spain and France. So named for La Madeleine, a cave in France.

MESOLITHIC: Middle Stone Age, following the Paleolithic. Although men were still hunters, cultivation of plants and animals was now begun. Lasted from about 8000 B.C. to about 5000 B.C. From the Greek, *Mesos*—middle, and *Lithos*—stone.

NEOLITHIC: New Stone Age. The culture following Mesolithic. Stone implements at their most developed. Domestication of animal and plant life well under way. In some parts of the world, isolated primitive peoples such as the American Indians and Australian aborigines still lived in Stone Age cultures until recently. In northern Europe, the Neolithic lasted from about 5000 B.C. to about 1500 B.C. From the Greek, *Neos*—new, and *Lithos*—stone.

PALEOLITHIC: Old Stone Age. The general name given to a period of several hundred thousand to two million years. All hominids who used stone tools are included in the Paleolithic, which is divided into two larger subdivisions, Lower and Upper. The Upper is the time of *Homo sapiens,* and is dated from about 35,000 to about 8000 B.C. Includes various cultures, such as Aurignacian, Magdalenian, etc. From the Greek, *Paleos*—old, and *Lithos*—stone.

FLINTS: hard stones, which when chipped and pointed, were used for tools, weapons, and fire making.

HOMINID: a man or manlike creature. From the Latin, *Homo*—man.

HOMO SAPIENS: man, the only surviving species. Literally, wise man. From the Latin, *Homo*—man, *Sapiens*—wise.

ICE AGES: periods when enormous sheets of ice covered large areas of the earth.

LEVEL: in archaeological excavation, a layer of earth that contains chiefly remains of one culture. Levels will be designated I, II, or III, etc., as different cultures are uncovered. Occasionally, artifacts or bones of level III may be found with level I, since items from culture I may have been used by people of culture III.

MAGDALENIAN: *see Culture*

MESOLITHIC: *see Culture*

MICROLITHS: very small stones, skillfully chipped and pointed for use as weapons or tools, set in larger tools. Used in the Upper Paleolithic in Europe and also later in other parts of the world. Probably used as arrows, as tips of spears, or as knives for skinning animals. From the Greek, *Micros*—tiny, and *Lithos*—stone. Sometimes used, incorrectly, to name all small stone implements.

NEOLITHIC: *see Culture*

PALEOLITHIC: *see Culture*

PLEISTOCENE: that period of geological time just before historical, or present times. Literally *most recent,* geologically speaking. Sometimes used as a synonym for ice ages. From the Greek, *Pleistos*—most, and *Cene*—recent.

PREHISTORY: the story of man's existence before writing was invented.

QUATERNARY: the fourth great geological era of the earth's existence. From the Latin, *Quaternius*—four together, or here, fourth in the order. The name is misleading, for the division into four eras is artificial. The only other such listing at present is Tertiary, or Third, the period just before, which started with the development of mammals on earth. Quaternary includes the Pleistocene and after.

STRATA: Beds or layers of rocks and earth. Each layer has its own geological characteristics, which help to identify it. From the Latin, *Stratum* —layer.

PHOTO CREDITS

Allied Chemical Corporation, p. 139

Ancora, Barcelona, COLOR PLATES 1, 2, 3, 4, 5, 6

Australian Museum, Sydney, Australia, p. 120, 127, 129

Centro Camuno di Studi Pristorici, Valcomonica, Italy, p. 38, 64, 73 (bottom)

C. K. Cooke, Director, Historical Monuments Commission, Rhodesia, COLOR PLATE 13

Ray Creeth, from C. K. Cooke, Director, Historical Monuments Commission, Rhodesia, p. 114

ENIT, from Italian Government Travel Office, New York, p. 58

ENIT, Rome, p. 62 (top), 65, 66

Professor Manuel Farinha dos Santos, from Casa de Portugal, New York, p. 22, 77

Feher, from French Government Tourist Office, New York, p. 50

Field Museum of Natural History, Chicago, p. xii, 4, 5, 11, 16 (top), 24, 30, 32, 42, 45, 46, 48, 53, 69, 70, 71, 74, 75

H. Frauca, from Australian News & Information Bureau, New York, p. 123

French Embassy Press and Information Division, New York, p. 20, 27, 104, 107

French Government Tourist Office, Chicago, COLOR PLATES 7, 8, 10, 11, 16

French Government Tourist Office, New York, COLOR PLATE 9

Frobenius Institute, Frankfurt am Main, Germany, p. 34, 37, 110, 112, 118, 119

Andrej Gavrjujov, Goteborg, Sweden, p. 86

Gourbeix, from French Government Tourist Office, Chicago, p. 54

Campbell Grant, Santa Barbara, California, p. 96, 100, COLOR PLATE 12

Professor Paolo Graziosi, Florence, Italy, p. 61, 62 (bottom)

George A. Laadt, Oak Park, Illinois, COLOR PLATE 15

Charles P. Mountford, St. Peters, South Australia, p. 124, 126

Tom Mulhern, from Campbell Grant, Santa Barbara, California, p. 94, 99

Museum of Modern Art, New York, from Frobenius Institute, Frankfurt am Main, Germany, p. viii, 39, 73 (top), 109, 113, 117

Musée de l'Homme, Paris, COLOR PLATE 14

National Park Service, Santa Fe, New Mexico, p. 102

Royal Norwegian Embassy Information Service, New York, p. 78, 81, 82, 83, 85

Soviet Embassy Information Service, Washington, D.C., from Novosti Press Agency, p. 88

Spanish Ministry of Information and Tourism, Madrid, p. 13, 31

Spanish National Tourist Office, Chicago, p. 8

P. Tarrosov, Soviet Peace Committee, Moscow, from Novosti Press Agency, p. 90, 91, 93

Fernand Windels, from French Government Tourist Office, Chicago, p. 28, 29

Yan, from French Government Tourist Office, New York, p. 16 (bottom), 25

INDEX

DOROTHY and JOSEPH SAMACHSON, as a team, have written books about the theater and the opera, archaeology and the city of Rome. She is also the author of a book about ballet, and he has published a book about the human skeletal system.

Mrs. Samachson is quite interested in music, having played piano in all kinds of places from the Metropolitan Opera in New York City to a supper club atop a Chicago hotel. Dr. Samachson, on the other hand, is a research organic chemist, who is now working with the Metabolic Research Unit of the Veterans Administration Hospital in Hines, Illinois.

Both of them are Easterners, Mrs. Samachson coming from New York and Dr. Samachson from New Jersey. They now make their home in Oak Park, Illinois. They are the parents of a son, Michael, and a daughter, Miriam, both of whom are married, and who share their parents' interest in music, literature, and science.